WHOSE BRIGHT IDEA WAS IT?

TRUE STORIES OF INVENTION

Larry Verstraete

Cover by Thomas Dannenberg
Design by Andrea Casault
Ilustrations by John Etheridge

Scholastic Canada Ltd.

Scholastic Canada Ltd.
123 Newkirk Road, Richmond Hill, Ontario Canada L4C 3G5

Scholastic Inc.
555 Broadway, New York NY 10012, USA

Scholastic Australia Pty Limited
PO Box 579, Gosford, NSW 2250, Australia

Ashton Scholastic Ltd.
Private Bag 579, Greenmount, Auckland, New Zealand

Scholastic Ltd.
Villiers House, Clarendon Avenue, Leamington Spa,
Warwickshire CV32 5PR, UK

Canadian Cataloguing in Publication Data

Verstraete, Larry
Whose bright idea was it? : True stories of invention

ISBN 0-590-24905-3

1. Toys - Juvenile literature. 2. Games - Juvenile literature.
I. Title.

TS2301.T7V47   j688.7'2   C96-931970

5 4 3 2 1   Printed in Canada   7 8 9/9

For young inventors everywhere
whose dreams today shape our world tomorrow.

Acknowledgements:

A special thanks to those who had a hand in
developing this book:
To colleague Jan Foster, for guiding me through
S.C.A.M.P.E.R. — the creative problem-solving
approach which became the basis for the Spotlight
sections in the book.
To Sandra Bogart Johnston, my editor at Scholastic
Canada, for her encouragement and wise counsel.
To my wife, Jo, and children, Stephen and Ashley, for
their suggestions, support, and patience.
And, especially, to the many inventors of the past . . .
without their legacy this book would not have been
possible.

Contents

Introduction

FOOD FAVOURITES

HOME HELPERS

PICTURE PERFECT

INFORMATION PLEASE

GAMES AND PUZZLES

INTRODUCTION

Inventions are everywhere.

Every day, we use dozens of devices and gadgets. Most of the time we don't give them a second thought. And maybe that's just as well. After all, inventions are supposed to make our lives easier, more efficient, or just plain fun.

But each invention has a story to tell.

Take the cereal you had for breakfast. Dr. John Kellogg discovered the secret to making crunchy flakes by accident. Rather than throw away a pot of mushy grain that had been cooked too long, Dr. Kellogg poured the sticky stuff into a pan and baked it in an oven. To his surprise — and our good fortune — the mixture broke into tasty flakes.

And your jeans? Those were Levi Strauss's idea. During the California Gold Rush, this young salesman bought bolts of canvas that he tried to sell as tents to prospectors. When the canvas didn't sell, Strauss sewed the material into pants, dyed them blue, then sold the sturdy clothing to the hard-working diggers. Today his "jeans" are worn by millions of people around the world.

The paper bag that holds your lunch? Give Margaret Knight credit for that. She invented the machinery that folds and glues the flat-bottomed bag. That's not Margaret's only invention, either. She came up with her first invention when she was only twelve, and during her lifetime she designed dozens of valves, rotors, engines and other machines.

This book is about the behind-the-scene stories of inventions you use each day.

Uncover fascinating facts and little-known stories about the things around you.

Read about inventors. Find out what inspired them. Learn about their triumphs and disasters.

Delve into their minds with the *Spotlight on Invention* sections that show how inventors think, create, and solve problems. Discover the secrets to their success and learn about other inventions that originated in the same way.

So read on . . . .

Who knows? Maybe you'll be inspired to follow the path of invention yourself.

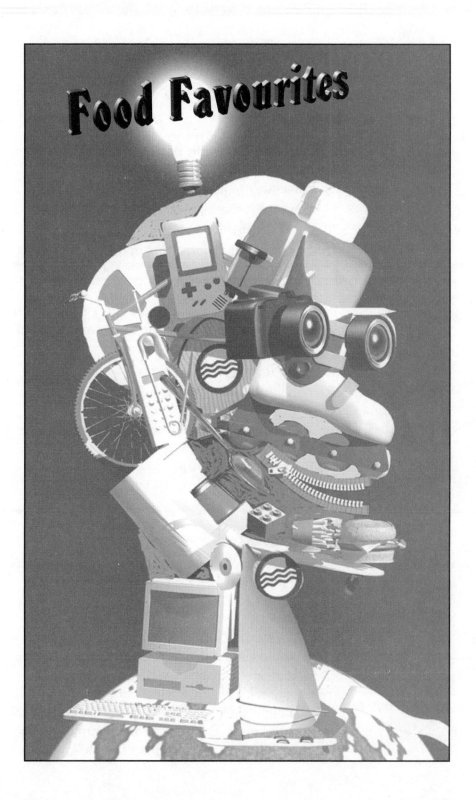

Food Favourites

FOOD FAVOURITES

Name These Foods:

1. George Crum wanted revenge on a complaining customer. Instead he produced this crispy, salty snack.

2. The Fleer brothers produced two versions of this treat. One coated his in candy. The other made sure his exploded at just the right moment.

3. Fourteen of the ingredients in this popular drink are known. The fifteenth is a tightly-guarded secret.

4. A small boy wanted chocolate and ice cream at the same time. Christian Nelson made this treat that had both.

5. When this jiggling, wiggling dessert was first introduced in 1895, hardly anyone wanted it. Today it's popular around the world.

6. This sweet popcorn and peanut treat comes with a prize in every box. Since 1912, over 1.7 billion have been given away.

Answers on page 23.

CEREAL FACTS

Although the Kelloggs were the first to produce cereal flakes, they weren't the first to invent dry breakfast cereal. In 1893 Henry D. Perky of Denver, Colorado, made a machine that shredded wheat and formed it into puffy biscuits. He called his cereal Shredded Wheat.

Besides cereal flakes, Dr. Kellogg deserves credit for other food inventions. In 1877 he invented granola. He also invented peanut butter, meat substitutes such as protose (for beef) and nuttose (for veal), and a grain substitute for coffee that he called Caramel Coffee. ➡

Breakfast Cereal

Millions of people start each day with a bowl of cereal flakes. John Harvey Kellogg would be pleased. So would Will Keith Kellogg. The two brothers invented the stuff.

In the late 1800s Dr. John Harvey Kellogg operated a medical boarding house in Battle Creek, Michigan. During their stay patients were expected to follow his prescription for health — plenty of fresh air, exercise, a good night's rest, and a diet free of coffee, alcohol, spices, and meat. Most people had no trouble with the fresh air and exercise parts of Dr. Kellogg's formula for good health. But to patients used to spicy meat dishes, vegetarian meals seemed bland.

Dr. Kellogg was always on the lookout for ways to make his food taste better. With his younger brother, Will Keith, he began experimenting with various foods. They spent evenings in the hospital kitchen boiling, mashing, and baking nuts and grains. Boiling, they knew, removed starch and created new flavours and textures. It also made grain gooey and gummy. But no matter how many times they tried, the Kelloggs were left with a sticky mess that baked into doughy globs.

One evening while they were boiling yet another batch of grain, the Kellogg brothers were called away on urgent business. They hurried out of the kitchen, leaving the pot to cool on the stove. By the time they got back to their experiment two days later, the over-boiled mush had started to dry and go mouldy.

Instead of throwing it out, they continued their experiment. They passed the dried dough through rollers to flatten it. To their surprise, each grain formed a separate flake, and each flake toasted evenly in the oven! With more experimenting the Kelloggs found the perfect formula for boiling and waiting that produced light, tasty — and unmouldy — flakes.

Dr. Kellogg was satisfied with the flakes purely from a health point of view. Not so with Will. He saw business opportunities in their discovery. Eventually he bought his brother's share of the flake invention, processed and packaged the cereal in Battle Creek, and created a breakfast food empire.

Bubble Gum

People, especially children, love to mangle and pop Frank Henry Fleer's invention — bubble gum!

The Aztec Indians of South America were the first

CEREAL FACTS

When the Kellogg Company celebrated its fiftieth anniversary in 1956, the city of Battle Creek staged a massive breakfast that has since become an annual tradition. Each June over 300 tables are set up along one of the town's main streets. Over 50,000 people enjoy free cereal, Pop-Tarts, doughnut holes, bananas, and milk at the world's longest breakfast table.

Today breakfast cereals are a billion-dollar industry and there are well over one hundred different brands on the market.

to discover the chewiness of chicle, the dried sap of a jungle tree. In the mid-1800s chicle was brought into the United States. Chicle itself was tasteless, but by adding flavours and syrups inventors improved the taste, and soon chewing gum became a favourite treat.

The pop and snap of chewing gum interested Frank Henry Fleer, an American inventor. He experimented with various formulas and in the early 1900s created a new gum that he called Blibber-Blubber Bubble Gum. Although kids took to Blibber-Blubber right away, the new gum had flaws. It burst before achieving a large bubble. And the gum was so wet it stuck to the face and was difficult to remove.

Blibber-Blubber was deemed a failure and was pulled off the market. But that didn't stop Frank Fleer. He continued to experiment and in 1928 introduced a stronger bubble gum called Dubble Bubble. Dubble Bubble made large, perfect bubbles. The new gum was "dry" too. When it popped, it peeled off easily.

Dubble Bubble was an instant success. But Frank Henry Fleer made the penny gum even more popular by selling it through another new invention, the vending machine.

At first, Fleer didn't think people would use vending machines. A machine salesman disagreed.

He said people would drop pennies into a machine even if there was nothing in it. To prove his point, he ran a most unusual test. He set up an empty vending machine just outside a busy building in New York City. The building was a popular place for tourists, but it was also one of the windiest spots in the city. The salesman set up a sign: "Drop a penny in the slot and listen to the wind blow."

Hundreds of people dropped pennies into the machine as they passed by. Finally, police arrived and shut down the operation, but not before the salesman had proved his point to an amazed Frank Fleer.

With his new improved bubble gum and the selling power of the vending machine, Fleer made bubble gum the snapping, popping favourite it remains today.

THE OTHER FLEER

The Other Fleer Frank Fleer wasn't the only family member to make chewing gum history. His brother, Henry, had a part too. While Frank busied himself looking for the perfect bubble gum recipe, Henry searched for the best candy-coated chewing gum.

One day in 1910 Henry had a measure of success. He managed to cover pellets of chicle with a brittle candy coating. In his excitement, the story goes, Henry dashed into Frank's office waving a handful of the white tablets and shouting, "Look, Frank — these little chiclets are coming along just fine!"

"That's it!" Frank answered, "That's what we'll call them — Chiclets!"

Chiclets were an instant success and have remained a top seller since that day.

GUM FACTS

A good bubble gum has to have just the right amount of "snap-back" or elasticity. Too little snap-back and a bubble bursts early and spreads over the chin and nose. With high snap-back the gum shrinks before it explodes, covering only the lips and saving the rest of the face from a mess.

Why is bubble gum almost always pink? According to some experts, the tradition started the day the first batch was made. Pink food colouring was the only one available on the factory shelves.

Chocolate Chip Cookie

Next time you bite into a chocolate chip cookie, thank Ruth Wakefield for taking a shortcut.

Ruth Wakefield and her husband Ken owned the Toll House Inn, a restaurant near Boston,

Massachusetts. One day in 1933 she decided to prepare a batch of cookies. The recipe called for chocolate. Wakefield wanted to save time, so instead of melting semi-sweet chocolate she broke the bar into pieces and tossed the bits into the batter, thinking that the chocolate would blend into the cookie dough as it baked. To her surprise and delight, the chocolate chunks softened slightly, but stayed whole.

Wakefield's "chocolate crispies" became a customer favourite at the Toll House Inn. As word spread, she started giving out her cookie recipe to anyone who was interested.

Meanwhile Nestlé, the chocolate manufacturer, noticed something odd. All across the country, sales of their semi-sweet chocolate bar had dropped. Everywhere, that is, except around Boston. Nestlé sent sales representatives to investigate. When Nestlé learned of the popular Toll House cookie, they decided to keep making the bars. They even tried to help out.

First they scored the bar so that it broke into pieces more easily. Then they invented a special chopper to break the chocolate into small bits. Finally, in 1939, they started marketing packages of chocolate chips just for cookie making. The company got permission to print Ruth Wakefield's Toll House Cookie Recipe on the package. In exchange, they supplied her with a lifetime's worth of free chocolate.

Two Other Cookie Favourites
Animal Crackers A popular Christmas gift for children in 1902 came without wheels or noise-makers. It wasn't soft or cuddly, either. But it could be eaten. And the small box it came in looked like a circus train. Animal Crackers!

Although the idea for animal-shaped cookies began in Britain, it was the National Biscuit Company (Nabisco) that gave Animal Crackers its unique package. Knowing how popular circus shows were for children, the company put the cookies in a small rectangular box printed to look like a circus train. A string handle made the box easy to carry, and encouraged parents to hang Animal Crackers on Christmas trees as gift decorations.

There may be another reason why Animal Crackers have always been a kid favourite. Parents report that children eat animal cookies in a disturbing way: first they nibble the back legs, then the front, then the head, and finally gobble down the rest of the body.

Oreo On April 2, 1912, Nabisco introduced three new cookies. Two were flops. The third, Oreo, was an immediate success.

From the start, cookie-lovers everywhere delighted in prying the wafers apart, licking the filling, then downing the rest. But why the name Oreo? No one knows for sure, but two guesses have been offered. Some believe Oreo comes from the Greek word *oros* which means mountain. Originally the cookie was to have had a peak, like a mountain top. Even though the final version of the cookie looked different, the name stuck. Others suggest that the name comes from *or,* which is French for gold, because the first packages had the cookie's name etched in gold letters.

The name may remain a mystery, but not the cookie's popularity. Over 5 billion Oreo cookies are eaten each year in the United States alone.

Cracker Jack

One of the taste treats sold at the Chicago World's Fair in 1893 was a mixture of popcorn, peanuts, and molasses. Inventor F.W. Rueckheim called his creation Cracker Jack.

After the fair, Rueckheim packaged Cracker Jack and started selling it in stores. People liked the sweetness and the crunchy flavour. In fact, one customer told Rueckheim, "The more you eat, the more you want." Rueckheim liked that phrase so much that he used it in his advertising.

Sales of Cracker Jack were steady, but they hit the roof when Rueckheim added a new gimmick in 1912. He packed a small toy in each box. Children loved munching their way through a box of Cracker Jack while searching for the treasure hidden inside.

Since that day over 17 billion toys have been given out as prizes, and so much Cracker Jack has been sold that if the boxes were placed end to end they would circle the world more than sixty-three times.

Coca-Cola

May 8, 1886, Atlanta, Georgia . . .

Pharmacist John Pemberton was experimenting in his backyard. His aim? To produce a new medicine that would help the nervous and exhausted to relax. In a brass kettle heated over an open fire Pemberton mixed caramel, coca leaves, cola nuts, fruit flavours and eleven other ingredients. He stirred the brew with a boat oar, tasting now and then, adding a pinch of this and that for flavouring.

When he finished, Pemberton had a thick dark syrup. He bottled a sample and rushed into a nearby pharmacy where he had his assistant mix it with water and ice. Both men agreed the new medicine tasted great. Sweet and delicious.

When Pemberton asked for a second round, however, his assistant goofed. Instead of adding plain water, he accidentally added carbonated water. The new batch tasted even better. That gave Pemberton an idea. Scrap plans to use the liquid as a medicine. Sell it as a beverage instead.

Calling the brew Coca-Cola after its two main ingredients — coca leaves and cola nuts — Pemberton managed to sell over one hundred litres of syrup around Atlanta the first year. In short order, though, sales skyrocketed. By 1895 Coca-Cola was being sold all across the United States. Today John Pemberton's soothing medicine has become the world's most popular soft drink.

Two Other Popular Drinks

Pepsi-Cola Pepsi-Cola was not an overnight success. Invented in 1898 by a North Carolina pharmacist, Caleb D. Bradham, the soda was called Brad's Drink. At first Bradham sold the brew only from drugstores, but people liked it so much that within a few years he was bottling it and selling it on a larger scale under the name Pepsi-Cola.

In 1920, Bradham made a colossal mistake. Thinking sugar prices were going to skyrocket, he bought huge quantities at about ten cents a kilogram. Instead of rising, however, sugar prices plummeted to less than two cents a kilogram just six months later. The company was almost wiped out.

In 1933, under new owners, Pepsi-Cola made a comeback. The company doubled the size of the bottle, offering twelve ounces (about 300 mL) of the drink for the same five cents that six ounces had once cost. Within two years, profits jumped to millions of dollars.

COCA-COLA FACTS

When customers nicknamed the drink Coke, the company was not pleased, but as more and more people asked for "a Coke" the company changed its mind. It registered the nickname, too, and in 1941 started using it in advertising.

Coca-Cola is sold in over 150 countries around the world, with sales of nearly 400 million drinks each day.

Hires Root Beer Sometimes ideas strike at the most unexpected times. Charles Elmer Hires, a chemist living in New Jersey, got his brain wave on his honeymoon.

In January, 1870, Hires married the daughter of a neighbour. That summer he took his bride for a short holiday. On the way the couple stopped for the night at a boarding house, where the landlady served them a homemade drink, a tea blended from roots, herbs and spices.

Hires had never tasted anything like it. When he got back home he experimented with different substances. He used the root of the sarsaparilla plant as his base and added other ingredients to sharpen its taste. But what to call this new drink? Hires thought the name root tea was just right. A friend disagreed. "They'll never drink it if you call it tea," he said. "Better call it root beer."

At first Hires sold the new beverage at the soda fountain in his own drugstore, but as it proved popular he expanded his business. In the 1880s he started selling packages of the ingredients (just add water, sugar and yeast, customers were told). Then, in 1893, Hires produced his first bottled root beer.

For over a hundred years Charles Hires's sarsaparilla mixture has been a favourite of young and old.

French Fries

One day in the 1830s, the story goes, a Belgian cook was preparing a stew. He cut potatoes into slices, but as he moved to toss them into a pot, he missed. The slices fell into a frying pan instead. No problem, the cook thought. I'll throw these out and start over with fresh potatoes. But there were no other potatoes, and without them the stew would be ruined.

Then a new and enticing aroma filled the kitchen. The potatoes in the frying pan smelled delicious. Perhaps, the cook thought, not all is lost. He served the fried potatoes and his guests loved their taste and crispy texture. When they asked the cook what he called the new dish, he answered in French, *"Pommes frites,"* which means fried potatoes.

News of the tasty food spread. Soon other people began to order French-style potatoes. Today we call them simply French fries.

Hamburger

Say the words "fast food" and most people think "hamburger." But the warlike tribes that invented hamburger weren't trying to save time at all. They were trying to make food easier to swallow.

Hundreds of years ago Mongolian and Turkish tribes known as Tartars shredded tough, low-quality meat to make it tender and easier to eat. Eventually the practice spread among other tribes.

In the fourteenth century Germans added spices to ground beef. In the town of Hamburg, the dish became known as the "Hamburg steak." When Germans immigrated to North America in the 1880s they brought the meat dish with them.

Just who invented the bun that comes with the modern hamburger is unknown. At least one vendor was selling hamburger sandwiches at the 1904 St. Louis World's Fair. Likely someone came up with the bright idea of putting the meat on a specially prepared roll at about the same time.

SPOTLIGHT ON INVENTION

Substitute One Thing for Another
to Create Something New

Everyone who has ever taken a shower has an idea. It's the person who does something about it who makes a difference.

— Nolan Bushnel,
inventor of Pong, the video game

THE HOT DOG STORY

How the Hot Dog Linked Up With the Bun

In 1904 a salesman named Anton Feuchtwanger set up a frankfurter booth at the World's Fair in St. Louis. When customers ordered a frankfurter — a long spicy sausage — Anton handed them a pair of white gloves to wear so their hands would be clean and grease-free. After they finished eating, customers were supposed to return the gloves, but many didn't, so Anton needed something to take their place. Something that didn't need to be returned. He asked his brother, a baker, to make longer-than-usual rolls. When someone ordered a frankfurter, he popped the meat onto the bun. No mess. No gloves. No returns. Soon everyone was selling frankfurters in buns.

But how did the frankfurter get to be called a "hot dog"? That too was a matter of one thing taking the place of another. Some people started calling the frankfurter the "dachshund sausage" because the long curved sausage reminded them of the dachshund — a long, lean dog. In 1906 a cartoonist named Tad Dorgan attended a baseball game in New York. He was fascinated by vendors shouting "Get your red hot dachshund dogs!" After the game Dorgan dashed to his office, and sketched a cartoon of a real-looking dachshund in a bun smeared with mustard. He couldn't spell dachshund so instead he wrote "Get your hot dogs!" The name stuck and is used to this day.

Other Substitution Inventions

Leotards In 1828 Nelson Hower, a bareback rider with the Buckley and Wicks Show, ran into a problem. His costume did not come back from the cleaners. Believing the show must go on at all costs, Hower did the best he could. He performed his act in his long underwear.

Other performers liked his idea and started wearing tight-fitting outfits too. One of them was Jules Leotard, a French trapeze artist. His performances were so thrilling, his one-piece outfits so unique, that his name became linked with the skin-tight clothing.

Paper Matches The first matches were awkward wooden sticks that were difficult to carry and to light. In 1889 Joshua Pusey, a Pennsylvania lawyer, improved the design by substituting paper for wood to make the matches smaller and lighter.

The idea of using paper matches didn't quite catch on, however, until 1897, when the Mendelssohn Opera Company decided to advertise an upcoming production in a new way. They printed their name on books of paper matches and passed them around. In no time, paper matches were a hit.

"Waffle" Soles When Bill Bowerman tried to make a new lightweight running shoe he found inspiration in the most unlikely place — the kitchen. Bowerman had been experimenting with rubber soles, and one morning as he sat at the kitchen table he stared at the open waffle iron. He had seen the waffle iron hundreds of times, but that day he noticed its grid-like pattern. Suddenly he had an idea.

What if he could make a lightweight sole with the same pattern as waffles? He experimented with liquid urethane, and finally produced a pad of square spikes made of hardened urethane.

Bowerman and his partner, Phil Knight, used the waffle design on their new running shoes. The shoes sold like hotcakes, and their company, Nike, stepped into running shoe history.

Ice Cream

No one is sure who first made ice cream. Or when it happened. Two thousand years ago, Roman Emperor Nero ordered slaves to bring him snow from the top of a nearby mountain. Nero flavoured the snow with fruit and honey and made himself one of history's first "water ices."

Over the centuries creative people added other ingredients to the icy mixture. Around 1600, adding cream became popular and the first of many different "cream ices" was born. Since then, inventors have stirred, whipped, and shaped ice cream into all kinds of delicious treats:

The name soda pop was given to carbonated drinks because of the popping sound the corks on their bottles made if they blew off.

Ice Cream Soda

Add syrup to cream and carbonated water . . .

So goes the simple recipe for a fizzy drink that was popular in the United States a century ago. Robert Green changed all that. He was an attendant at a large celebration in Philadelphia in 1874. Partway through the party he ran short of cream for his fizzy drinks. In its place he added a scoop of vanilla ice cream. The mixture fizzed and foamed and became an instant hit.

Ice Cream Sundae

A man named Smithson had a food bar in his store in Wisconsin. People often dropped around for a refreshing dish of ice cream. On one particular Sunday in 1890, Smithson ran into a problem. He started running low on ice cream. He had lots of other supplies, though — fruit, some chocolate syrup, and some heavy cream — but little ice cream.

Since there were no deliveries on Sunday, Smithson did the best he could with what he had. He served smaller portions of ice cream and topped them with fruit, chocolate syrup, and whipped cream.

People loved Smithson's creation. Word got around and soon others started asking for the "Sunday ice cream" on other days of the week. Not everyone liked the name for the new dessert, though. Some thought using the word Sunday, the Lord's day, was wrong, so Smithson changed the spelling to "sundae."

Ice Cream Cone

The exact story behind the invention of the ice cream cone is somewhat of a mystery. One thing is certain, however. The ice cream cone was invented in 1904 at the St. Louis World's Fair.

Two men at the fair had side-by-side fast food booths. One sold ice cream in paper dishes. The other, Ernest Hamwi, sold zalabia, a waffle-like pastry sprinkled with sugar.

August was hot. Cool treats were in big demand, and the ice cream salesman did a booming business.

One scorching day, he sold so much ice cream that by noon he had run out of dishes. Without dishes, he would have to close his booth and lose half a day's business.

According to one version of the story, Hamwi came to his rescue. He rolled a warm waffle into a cone shape, let it cool and harden, then passed it to his neighbour, who scooped ice cream on top.

Other versions credit an ice cream salesman with the invention of the cone. Still others say it was the salesman's girlfriend who happened to be helping him out. Whatever the story, people at the fair loved the cool and crisp combination. The treat became so popular that by 1920 one-third of all ice cream consumed in the United States was eaten from cones!

Ice Cream Bar

A young boy with a difficult decision gave Christian Nelson his bright idea.

Nelson owned an ice cream and candy store in Onowa, Iowa. One day a boy came into the store, clutching a few coins in his hand. At first he asked for a chocolate bar. Then he changed his mind. No, he decided, make that an ice cream sandwich.

Nelson started to cut a slice of ice cream, preparing to put it between two wafers, when the boy changed his mind again. No, he wanted the chocolate bar after all.

The incident stuck with Christian Nelson for some time. It seemed that neither the chocolate bar nor the ice cream sandwich could make the boy entirely happy. Why couldn't he have both? Why not freeze a chocolate coating around a slice of ice cream?

Using every spare minute he could find, Christian Nelson experimented with mixtures of chocolate and ice cream in a back room of his store. The idea was

When Cheerios were first marketed in 1941, they were called Cheery Oats.

simple enough, but doing it was tricky. No matter what he tried, the chocolate wouldn't stick to the ice cream.

One day he mentioned his problem to a candy salesman. Chocolate candy manufacturers, the salesman explained, use cocoa butter to make chocolate stick to the candy centres. So Nelson tried again, but this time he changed the quantities of cocoa butter. Late one night in 1920 he dipped a slice of ice cream into a heated chocolate mixture, and the chocolate coating solidified onto the ice cream bar.

The chocolate coating was a great success, and Christian Nelson became a wealthy man, thanks to a small boy and his very difficult decision.

JELL-O

JELL-O is one of North America's favourites, but it wasn't always such a popular treat.

Back in 1642 a Frenchman, Denis Papin, discovered that by boiling animal bones he could remove a jelly-like material that he called gelatin. It had no colour, no odour, no flavour, and few practical uses.

In 1895 an American cough syrup manufacturer named Pearl B. Wait added fruit syrup to gelatin. His wife, Mary, took one look at the quivering mass and called it JELL-O. The name stuck, but when Wait tried to sell JELL-O no one wanted it. The dessert was too strange and unusual for most people's tastes.

After four frustrating years of trying to sell JELL-O, Wait gave up. He sold the product rights to a cereal manufacturer, Orator Woodward. At first Woodward didn't have any more success than Wait. Stacks of unsold JELL-O filled warehouses, and at one point he tried to unload the whole business on a friend for only thirty-five dollars.

Then around 1900 a number of cooks decided that

JELL-O was just the perfect ending to an elegant meal. It began appearing at banquets and in fancy restaurants. Suddenly sales of the dessert that no one had wanted boomed. By 1906 Woodward was selling nearly a million dollars' worth a year.

Potato Chips

Revenge was all George Crum really wanted. Instead, he produced this tasty snack.

Crum was a chef at the Moon Lake Lodge, a resort in Saratoga Springs, New York. One day in 1853 an unhappy guest sent his order of French fries back to the kitchen. "Make them thinner, saltier and crispier," he commanded.

Crum steamed at the complaint. After all, he had made delicious French fries hundreds of times before. Reluctantly he tried again, but the second batch was returned, too. Not one to give up, Crum whipped up a new batch of thinner, well-fried slices. Once again the hard-to-please customer rejected them.

In a huff the frazzled chef seized a potato and cut it into slices so thin you could see through them. He soaked the slices in ice-cold water, then fried them crispy brown and salted them heavily. With a great deal of show he marched into the dining room and set the paper-thin slices before the startled guest, satisfied that revenge was his at last. The customer was sure to hate these overdone, over-salted potatoes.

As Crum stood smiling, the guest took a bite. The crunchy slice melted in his mouth. He savoured the taste. To Crum's amazement the guest congratulated him on his outstanding new dish.

The very next day "George Crum's Saratoga Chips" appeared on the restaurant menu. As their popularity grew, their name was changed, though. Today we call them simply "potato chips."

SPOTLIGHT ON INVENTION

Reverse, Rearrange, or Reorder
to Make Something Better

*Our heads are round so that our thinking can
change direction.*

— Francis Picabia

THE PRINGLES STORY

How Thinking Backwards Saved the Day

How do you package fragile potato chips so that they
arrive fresh and unbroken? Many manufacturers add air or
other gases to the package, fluffing it up so that the chips
are less likely to be crushed. That creates a second
problem: space. Bigger bags take more room.

The Proctor and Gamble Company looked at the packaging
problem from all angles and found a solution in a most
unlikely place. Under a tree.

As one employee watched leaves falling from a tree, he
noticed that while fresh wet leaves lay undisturbed on the
ground, dry leaves crumbled easily. The leaves reminded
him of thin potato slices . . . and that gave him an idea.

Usually, potato chips are processed and dried before
packaging. The employee reversed the process. He stacked
wet potato slices in a tube-like container and dried them
later. Unlike regular potato chips,
the new chips kept their uniform
shape, did not crumble, and
could be packaged more
compactly than those in bags.

The company loved the idea
and a new chip was born:
Pringles.

Other Inventions Created by Reversing, Rearranging, or Reordering

Flashlight Joshua Lionel Cowen invented an unusual flowerpot that had a battery and small light bulb in it. When a button was pressed, light travelled up a tube in the pot and illuminated the flower. The lighted flowerpot never caught on, so Cowen sold the rights for almost nothing to a friend, Conrad Hubert. Hubert dismantled the pot and remade the battery, bulb, and tube into an "electric hand torch." The flashlight proved popular and by the time of his death in 1928, Hubert was worth millions. (Cowen had his own measure of success, too. He invented the model train and started the Lionel Train Company. See page 111.)

Self-Service Shopping At one time shoppers in grocery stores ordered items at a front counter and waited while clerks gathered the goods. To Clarence Saunders, a grocery store operator in Memphis, Tennessee, this seemed inefficient and time-consuming. Why not reverse the process? he thought. Why not let customers select their own items, then pay for them later at the counter?

In 1916 Saunders reorganized his store, widening the aisles and adding handy baskets for his customers to use. Self-service shopping proved so popular that Saunders opened a second store five weeks later.

Vacuum Cleaner Cecil Booth's brainwave came after he watched another inventor demonstrate a dust-removing machine that forced compressed air into a carpet. Booth noticed that more dust was spread than was collected, so he reversed the process. Rather than forcing air *into* the carpet, he created a machine that sucked air out. His suction machine was the forerunner of the modern vacuum cleaner.

Sandwich

Call them subs, heroes, sloppy joes, hoagies — they're sandwiches by any name.

A wealthy Englishman named John Montagu created the very first one. Montagu loved to gamble. He spent so many hours at gaming tables that he often missed meals and sleep. One day in 1762 he became deeply involved in a card game. The game had already lasted twenty-four hours, and although Montagu was hungry, he wasn't about to leave the table.

He ordered a servant to bring him meat and bread. He picked up a slice of bread, topped it with a thick slab of meat, then put another slice of bread on top of it. Holding the food in one hand, Montagu used his free hand to play cards.

Montagu's gambling friends started copying his idea, and named the new food after its inventor: John Montagu, the Earl of Sandwich.

OTHER FOOD BITS

Doughnuts

One interesting legend has it that the round doughnut with the centre hole was invented during a violent ocean storm. Hanson Gregory, a nineteenth-century sea captain, was eating a doughy, sweet fried bread when the ship lurched suddenly, pitching him against the ship's wheel and lodging the snack on one of the wheel's spokes. With the bread now firmly in place, Gregory's hands were free to steer the ship. Later, he ordered holes in all his sweet breads, and the doughnut was created.

Gatorade
During a football game players sweat, and sometimes lose close to seven kilograms. In the final quarter they often hit a slump as their energy dwindles. Those facts started James Robert Cade, a kidney researcher at the University of Florida, thinking. Cade analyzed sweat and found that it contained water, sodium, potassium, and other important minerals. He whipped up a lime-flavoured liquid that contained concentrations of the missing nutrients. When the University of Florida Gators drank Cade's concoction, they felt less exhausted midway through the game. Eventually, Cade sold his formula — now nicknamed Gatorade — to a bottling company. Today Gatorade is used by sports teams around the world.

Lifesavers
When sales of chocolate candies were slow in the summer of 1912, candymaker Clarence A. Crane tried manufacturing mints instead. Crane convinced a pill-maker to use his machinery to press out the candy. The machinery punched a hole in the centre of each mint, making it look just like a miniature life-preserver. The name Lifesavers seemed perfect!

Pizza

Think pizza, and likely you think Italian. Wrong! The first pizzas were actually invented by the ancient Greeks, who made an assortment of flat breads topped with vegetables, herbs, and spices. The idea spread across continents, but it wasn't until 1889 that

tomatoes were first added. Raffaele Esposito wanted to make a specially coloured pizza to honour Italian Queen Margherita. He chose mozzarella cheese and basil to represent white and green (two colours of the Italian flag) then added tomatoes for red, the third and final colour.

Popcorn

With butter or plain? Hot air or microwaved? Whatever its form, popcorn has been around a long time. Archeologists found 5600-year-old popcorn in Bat Cave in New Mexico, proving that it was an early favourite of native North American people. Later European explorers discovered popcorn for themselves and brought the food back home for others to sample.

Jacob Beresin started the custom of eating popcorn in movie theatres. Beresin worked at the Metropolitan Opera House in Philadelphia. To earn extra money he sold popcorn and other snacks during intermissions. The idea caught on, and soon Beresin and his partner were selling snacks in all nine of Philadelphia's theatres. As their business boomed, the idea spread to numerous other cities.

When butter grew scarce in the 1860s, the French government offered a prize for the best "cheap butter." The result? Margarine!

Pretzels

Legend has it that pretzels were invented in the Middle Ages by an Italian monk, to reward children who memorized their prayers. After rolling bread dough into long strands, the monk twisted them so that they looked like arms crossed in prayer. He salted and baked them, then passed them out as treats to worthy children.

Answers To Name These Foods. . .
1. Potato chips 2. Both produced chewing gum. Henry Fleer invented Chiclets. Frank Fleer invented bubble gum. 3. Coca-Cola 4. The ice-cream bar 5. JELL-O 6. Cracker Jack

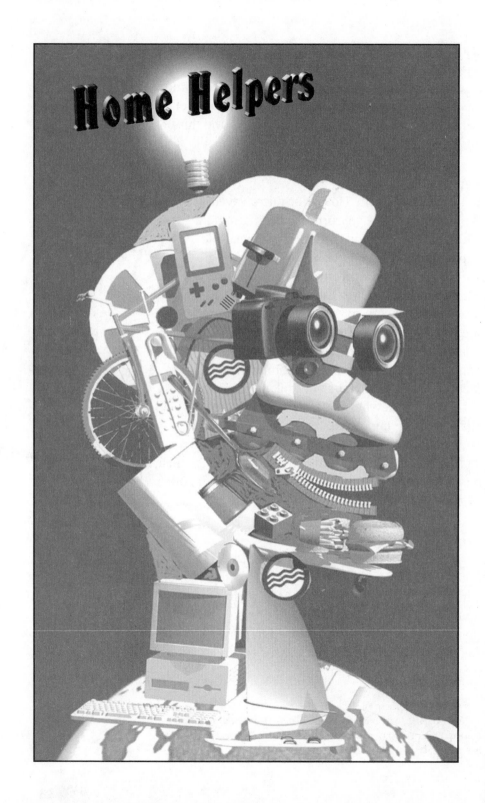

HOME HELPERS

Name These Home Appliances or Machines:

1. A gooey candy bar gave Percy Spencer the idea, but exploding eggs and popcorn proved it worked. Thanks to Spencer's experiments, millions around the world cook their food faster than ever before.

2. As Edwin Budding watched the spinning blades of a shearing machine cut fibres in a carpet factory, he got the idea to build a similar device for outdoor use at home.

Answers on page 38.

Dishwasher

Josephine Cochrane was fed up. Fed up with broken dishes. Fed up with the servants who washed them. Even fed up with the mail service that took months to ship expensive new china to replace the old. She was so annoyed with her shattered dishes that she vowed to do something about it.

One day in 1866 she gathered her china and headed to a woodshed near her home in Shelbyville, Illinois. Using heavy wire she constructed individual compartments to hold each cup, saucer and plate. Next she fastened the wire compartments around a wheel, and fixed the wheel inside a huge copper drum. Hot soapy water spurted from the bottom, washing grease and food bits off the dishes.

Cochrane's wealthy friends were impressed. So were nearby hotels and restaurants. In December, 1886, she patented her invention and started a company to manufacture dishwashers. For years, restaurants and hotels remained her best customers. Then in 1914 her company started building smaller

Christopher Latham Sholes got the idea for a typewriter keyboard after watching a concert pianist.

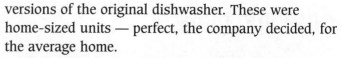

versions of the original dishwasher. These were home-sized units — perfect, the company decided, for the average home.

But the first home dishwashers did not sell. One reason was lack of hot water. In 1914 home water tanks were small, and slow to heat. A dishwasher might use the entire hot water supply to do a single load. Also, most homes used hard water containing dissolved minerals that clogged openings and prevented soap from sudsing the way it should. In 1932 the first dishwashing detergent, Calgon, hit the market. Its sudsing power and ability to rinse dishes clean solved some of the hard water problems.

Another reason the home dishwasher sold poorly at first was that Josephine Cochrane, the lady who never washed dishes herself, figured dishwashing was a disagreeable chore. But many housewives of the day enjoyed washing dishes and found it relaxing. Forty years later things changed. In the 1950s, as more women worked outside the home and leisure time became a greater concern, demand for home dishwashers increased.

Drip Coffee Maker

People have been drinking coffee since A.D. 800, but it took until 1908 for someone to come up with a better way to make it. Melitta Bentz, a German housewife, always prepared her coffee the way others did. First she wrapped the ground beans in a small bag. Then she popped the bag into a pot of water and boiled it. The result? A bitter-tasting liquid swimming with loose coffee grounds.

Bentz thought there had to be a faster way to make better-tasting coffee. One day she cut a circle from a sheet of blotting paper, found a brass pot, poked small holes into the bottom, and placed the paper inside. She put coffee grounds on top of the paper,

---

COFFEE FACTS

Legend has it that coffee was first discovered by an Ethiopian goatherd named Kaldi. He noticed that each time his goats ate the bright red berries that grew on a certain type of bush, they became restless and frisky. One night, in an effort to stay awake as he guarded the herd, Kaldi tried the berries himself. They were too hard to chew, so he boiled them and drank the brown liquid. Before long he felt perky and wide awake. Kaldi took the berries home, shared them with others in the village, and started a new beverage tradition.

The word "coffee" is derived from Kava, the name of Kaldi's village. Over time Kava became *café* in French and Spanish, *kaffee* in German, *kofe* in Russian, and coffee in English.

then poured boiling water over them. The water slowly seeped through the grounds and out the bottom of the pot. The coffee tasted rich and full, with none of its traditional bitterness. The paper caught most of the loose grounds, too, preventing them from spoiling the flavour.

Melitta Bentz was impressed. So was her husband, Hugo. They hired a tinsmith to make coffee pots with dozens of small holes in the bottom, and went into business selling them. They called their invention the Melitta coffeemaker.

In 1909 the Bentzes introduced their product at a local trade show. It was an instant success: over 1200 coffeemakers were sold in a matter of days. Today, some 90 years after Melitta Bentz first tried her invention, millions of people in 150 countries around the world use her drip method to prepare fresh, rich-tasting coffee.

Lawn Mower

Edwin Budding worked at an English factory that made carpets. But Budding had more than his job on his mind, it would appear: namely, the grass he had to cut at home. Grass cutting in the early 1800s was difficult and tedious. First the grass had to be dampened to give it "body." Then a heavy, long-handled blade called a scythe was swung through the grass to trim it. Cutting grass in the hot summer sun was hard work, and Budding dreaded it.

As he brooded over the chore he noticed a new machine in the factory. Known as a rotary shearer, the machine's spinning blades cropped excess fibres from carpets. Budding

wondered if the machine would work on grass too. At home, he built a push mower. He fastened several rotary blades to a set of wheels. As the wheels turned the blades rotated, trapping grass against a fixed cutter and trimming it.

With Budding's mower a difficult job was made much easier, and since the mower worked on dry grass, time was saved as well. But despite its advantages the push mower never gained popularity in Budding's lifetime. Fifty years later, however, when prices of the mower dropped and carefully groomed lawns became important status symbols, his invention could be found in toolsheds everywhere.

After golfers noticed that old, dented balls flew farther than new, smooth ones, manufacturers started making dimpled golf balls. Regulation golf balls have 336 dimples.

More Power To You, Edwin!

Edwin George, an American army colonel in the early 1900s, had his eye on his wife's washing machine. Not that George was worried about clean clothes. It was the gasoline motor on the washing machine that he wanted.

George used a push mower to cut grass, but when he noticed the washing machine at work, he had an idea. He took the motor off the washing machine and fastened it to the mower. As the motor chugged, it turned the cutting blades. Now instead of pushing and straining, George simply guided the mower around the yard, letting the motor do the work of trimming the grass.

Although the gasoline-powered lawn mower revolutionized grass cutting, history does not tell us what Mrs. George thought of her husband's brainstorm.

SPOTLIGHT ON INVENTION

Take Advantage of the Unexpected

Originality is simply a fresh pair of eyes.
— Woodrow Wilson

Name the greatest of all inventors: Accident.
— Mark Twain

THE STORY OF THE MICROWAVE OVEN

How a Surprise Discovery Changed the Way We Cook

A candy bar changed our world in a way no one could have predicted.

In 1946 a British engineer, Percy L. Spencer, was hard at work on a radar set when he reached into his pocket for a snack. Instead of a chocolate bar, he discovered a soft, gooey mess. He was curious. The room had not been especially warm. What had caused the chocolate to melt?

The firm Spencer worked for, Raytheon Manufacturing Company, made radar sets for the British military. Spencer had been working close to a magnetron, the power tube that drives a radar set. The messy candy bar got Spencer thinking. Working on a hunch, he sent for a bag of popcorn and held the unpopped kernels next to the magnetron. Within minutes, kernels exploded over the laboratory floor.

The next morning Spencer brought a tea kettle and a few raw eggs to work. He cut a hole in the side of the kettle, placed an uncooked egg inside, and pointed the hole towards the magnetron. In seconds the egg exploded. Bits of shell and yolk fired out of the kettle, splattering the face of another engineer who had stood too close.

Now Spencer was convinced. Short radio waves — or microwaves — produced by the magnetron had been the cause. If microwaves cooked eggs quickly, why not other foods?

MICROWAVE FACTS

Microwaves cause water molecules in food to vibrate. The hot water molecules then spread heat to surrounding molecules. A kernel of corn pops because the water at its centre heats quickly and expands. Raw eggs explode because water inside changes to steam, causing heat and pressure to build inside the shell. Since only water molecules are affected by microwaves, materials such as glass, paper, and plastic can be placed in a microwave oven without being damaged. ➡

 29

Spencer demonstrated his experiment to Raytheon officials, who then set out to produce a microwave-powered cooking device. In early 1953 the first microwave oven hit the marketplace. Weighing almost 340 kilograms and the size of a refrigerator, the "Radarange" was too bulky and expensive ($3000) for household use. It was sold to restaurants, hotels, and railroads.

Over the next two decades improvements were made to the microwave oven. The magnetron became smaller and simpler. It was hidden at the back of the oven and pipes led waves to the food. Now the size of a television set, the new microwave oven could be stored on a kitchen counter. Most importantly, it was affordable — less than $500. Today more homes have microwave ovens than dishwashers, and steaming hot food is ready for the table in minutes, thanks to a messy chocolate bar and Percy Spencer's curiosity.

MICROWAVE FACTS

Metals cause microwaves to reflect inside the oven, causing a build-up that eventually produces sparks and could cause fires.

Percy Spencer, a self-educated man who never finished elementary school, patented 120 inventions during the 39 years he worked with Raytheon.

Other Inventions Produced By Unexpected Results

Ivory Soap In 1878 a worker for the Proctor and Gamble Company accidentally left a batch of soap stirring in a vat while he had lunch. Afraid to admit his mistake, he shipped out the soap anyway. Soon the company received orders for "the soap that floats." The overstirring had trapped air in the soap, causing it to float on water instead of sinking like other soaps. To meet the demand the company started production of Ivory Soap.
Scotchgard Chemist Patsy Sherman accidentally spilled a chemical on her tennis shoe in 1973. She noticed that while the rest of her shoe got dirty, the spot where the chemical had fallen remained clean. Eventually her curiosity led to the development of a new stain-resistant mixture, Scotchgard.

Teflon In 1938 Roy Plunkett, a chemist for the Du Pont company, was searching for a new type of refrigerator coolant. He opened the valve to a full tank of gas, but nothing came out. Surprised, Plunkett sawed open the cylinder and found a waxy white powder inside. It was slippery and not affected by ordinary chemicals. Plunkett named the material Teflon, short for its lengthy chemical name, tetrafluoroethylene. Today Teflon is used on frying pans, but has dozens of other applications as well, from heat shields on rockets to coatings on light bulbs that reduce shattering.

See Also:
Breakfast Cereal (page 2)
Post-Its (page 140)
Slinky (page 110)

Breakfast Cereal (page 2)
Post-Its (page 140)
Slinky (page 110)

TOASTER FACTS

People have been toasting bread for thousands of years. For the ancient Egyptians it was a convenient way to preserve food. With moisture removed, bread grew less mould and lasted longer.

The first one hundred pop-up toasters Charles Strite made were failures, but once he perfected his invention chefs came to love it. Why? No longer having to keep watch over the toaster, they were free to work at other things.

Pop-Up Toaster

Charles Strite, a mechanic working in a plant in Stillwater, Minnesota, often ate in the company cafeteria. One day in 1919 he ordered toast. A hard, blackened slice of bread arrived on a plate. Frustrated with his charred meal, Strite decided to take matters into his own hands.

Electric toasters had been around since 1909, but they were simple things, a few bare wires wrapped around insulating strips of mica. They heated only one side of bread at a time, and lacked heat controls, so the bread had to be watched constantly and snatched out of the toaster the instant it was ready, or else it burned.

In his home workshop Strite tinkered with wires and springs. When he was finished, he had a new, improved toaster. Unlike earlier models, this toaster heated the bread on both sides at the same time. It used a timing device, too, in combination with springs. When the toast was ready, the mechanism cut off the power and the toast popped up.

At first Strite sold his invention only to hotels and restaurants. Then in 1927 a home version hit the marketplace. Called the Toastmaster, it promised effort-free perfect toast. According to a newspaper advertisement of the time, "This amazing new invention makes perfect toast every time! Without watching! Without turning! Without burning!"

Not quite true, however. While the first slice toasted evenly, the following slices grew darker and darker as the toaster's temperature got hotter and hotter. The problem was finally corrected in 1930 when a thermostat was added.

Refrigerator

Ever drop a bit of rubbing alcohol on your hand? Rubbing alcohol evaporates quickly, making the skin feel cool. Nail polish remover works the same way. Both are volatile liquids.

Jacob Perkins, an American who lived in Britain in 1834, was one of the first people to notice the cooling effect of volatile liquids. He wondered what would happen if he enclosed volatile liquids in metal tubes. He figured that the liquids would evaporate, cooling down both the tubes and the air around them.

Perkins and a group of friends built a small box, wound metal tubes through it, sealed a volatile liquid inside and rigged up a pump to compress the liquid and keep it flowing. The device worked. As the story goes, Perkins put a tray of water inside the box. In time the box cooled and turned the water into ice. Perkins and his friends were so excited that they wrapped the ice in a blanket, flagged down a cab, and headed to Perkins's house to celebrate.

REFRIGERATION FACT

The principle of refrigeration may have been invented by the Chinese hundreds of years ago. The Chinese used salt water or brine to preserve foods. Heated brine evaporates quickly, causing a cooling effect. The Chinese may have noticed this cooling effect, and used brine as a refrigerant.

Although Perkins was among the first to build a successful refrigerator, he did not develop his invention. He seemed to be satisfied just knowing that it worked. In 1855 another inventor, James Harrison, designed and marketed the first industrial refrigerator to harness the cooling effect of volatile liquids. Other inventors followed, and by the early 1900s household refrigeration units began appearing in stores around the country.

Sewing Machine

If ever there was a tale of rags to riches, it is the story of Elias Howe Jr.

Howe worked in a Boston machine shop. One day in 1839 he overheard an argument between the owner and another worker. "Why waste time on a knitting machine?" the owner said. "Invent a sewing machine and you'll make a fortune." To the penniless Howe, who earned only two or three dollars a week, these words seemed like magic. A fortune, just for a machine that sewed!

At first, Howe tried making a machine that duplicated the movements used in sewing. He observed his wife sewing, but the movements were too complicated for a machine to copy. So he changed his approach. He devised a new kind of stitch, simpler in design and more easily duplicated by machine. But even with this improvement he had not built a workable sewing machine.

Then one day as he was repairing a watch he noticed that many parts of the watch moved at the same time. That's just what his machine needed, he realized, two needles working together at the same time: one moving up and down to make a loop stitch, the other moving across to draw thread through the loop.

On another occasion Howe dreamed of a

SEWING MACHINE FACTS

An experienced tailor sewing by hand could make thirty stitches in a minute. Howe's machine could make 250 in the same time.

Although Howe invented the first successful double-thread lock-stitch machine, a French tailor named Barthelemy Thimmonier had invented a simpler single-thread machine sixteen years earlier. The machine had a short life. Local tailors who figured they were losing business because of the invention charged through Thimmonier's sewing factory, destroying all the machines and nearly killing him as well. ➡

strange arrow with a hole in the shaft near its tip. He jolted awake, suddenly understanding what he had seen in the dream. The arrow was like a needle, only the eye of this needle was near its point, not at the opposite end like regular needles. Howe added this feature to his machine.

After seven years of struggle Howe had finally created a machine that sewed in straight even stitches, but it was expensive, $300, and not very efficient. American manufacturers refused to carry it. Frustrated, Howe took his machine and moved his family to England. Two years later he returned, poorer than ever. To his surprise he found sewing machines very much like his own selling in stores for $100. Others, he thought, had stolen his invention.

He went through a long, costly court battle. In the end the judge decided that Howe was the original inventor of the sewing machine, and that each manufacturer owed him a royalty for every machine made. Howe became very rich very quickly, collecting royalties of more than $4000 a week, but misfortune continued to plague him. His wife died before he earned a penny from his invention, and he himself died when he was only forty-eight.

ISAAC SINGER

Everyone Needs a Singer

It was Elias Howe Jr. who invented the sewing machine, but Isaac Singer who put it into homes around the globe. In 1850, while Howe was in England, Singer spotted several copies of Howe's sewing machine around Boston. None of them worked well, but Singer immediately saw ways to make them better. He straightened out the curved needle, made it move up and down instead of horizontally, added an adjustable lever to hold fabric in place, and used a foot-operated treadle to free the sewer's hands. But despite these differences, Singer's machine formed the same stitch as Howe's so he had to pay Howe a royalty for each machine made.

Although Singer was a capable inventor, he was an even better salesman. He hatched an elaborate scheme to sell his machine. "Come and see a machine sew a pair of trousers in forty minutes!" said his ads. Then he stationed attractive young women at Singer sewing machines in shop windows around town. People flocked to the demonstrations and gawked to see a pair of pants whipped up in minutes.

Then Singer went a step further. He sent teams of salesmen door to door, each one trained to demonstrate the product in any home. He offered a sales plan, too. Purchasers could buy on installment by putting a small amount down, then paying a reasonable amount each month until the account was settled. To service the machines, Singer trained a fleet of mechanics and set up conveniently located repair shops. Sales of Singer sewing machines boomed.

The sewing machine changed the lives of housewives around the globe. It also changed the life of Isaac Singer. He became so wealthy that in his later years he retired to England and built a palace complete with marble columns and an indoor theatre.

Snowblower

In Quebec, where Arthur Sicard lived, snow fell in heaps, often plugging roads and stopping traffic. Sicard aimed to do something about the problem.

When he was eighteen, Sicard spotted a new machine, a thresher. As it moved across the field, its long spinning blades turned, cutting stalks of grain. Sicard saw the possibilities. On his own he built a snow removing machine with features similar to the thresher. Its blades churned up snow and spewed it out through a chute. Sometimes it stalled and became snagged in large drifts, but he knew he could modify and improve it with time and money.

Sicard was the talk of the town. People thought he was mad. Even his friends and neighbours shunned him. When he approached them for financial support, they refused to help. Not one to give up, Arthur Sicard left home, moved to Montreal, found a job in the construction industry, and worked until he had enough money to continue with his dream.

He bought an old truck, removed its bumpers, and in their place attached two rotating blades and a long chute. Behind the cab he added an extra motor to power the blades. In 1925 he took his improved model to the snow-plugged streets. The blades turned, chewing up even the heaviest drifts, leaving a clear path behind the truck.

Once again Sicard was the talk of the town. This time people wanted to know where they could get such a machine for themselves. Towns across Quebec placed orders for Sicard's snow-clearing invention. Eventually smaller, more portable models were available for homeowners too. Today, in snowbound countries around the world, Arthur Sicard's invention is at work clearing streets, sidewalks and driveways.

MORE HELPFUL BITS

Not everything that's helpful around the home is big, complicated, or needs to be plugged in or turned on. Where would we be without simple but useful inventions such as these?

S.O.S Pads

Edwin Cox needed a gimmick.

Cox was a door-to-door salesman who peddled pots and pans. But sales were poor and he had difficulty even getting his foot inside most doors. What he needed, he thought, was a free introductory gift, a simple but useful object he could give to customers for allowing him to show his cookware.

Cox thought long and hard. Most of his customers were homemakers. Many complained about cleaning stuck-on food from pans. A new cleaning pad seemed like the perfect gift.

In his kitchen, Cox soaked small squares of steel wool in a soapy solution. He let the pads dry, then redipped and dried them over and over until each pad was filled with dried soap. When he went knocking on doors again, he offered each customer one free pad. Sales of cookware increased, but so did demand for the soapy pads. People loved the scratchy cleaners and wanted more. Before long Cox stopped selling pots and pans. He devoted all his time to making and selling soap pads. But he needed a name for his product. His wife called them S.O.S for "Save Our Saucepans." S.O.S seemed simple, yet catchy — the perfect choice.

WD-40

Got a squeaky door? How about a stubborn crayon mark on the wall? A wad of gum in the carpet? Reach for WD-40. Many people claim this spray-on lubricant works wonders on rusty metal parts and removes stains and goo from all sorts of unlikely places.

WD-40 got its start in unusual circumstances. In 1952 an airplane manufacturer stored several new jet planes on a runway in San Diego. Over the damp winter the planes began to rust. Realizing that millions of dollars of airplanes were in danger of rusting to pieces, the manufacturer sought help from Rocket Chemical, a small lubricant company. Head chemist Norman Larsen knew what was needed: a new product that seeped into the metal, pushed out water, and coated the surface to protect it from rust.

Larsen whipped up a batch of chemicals. After running some tests he shipped a sample to the airplane manufacturer. It was rejected. Larsen tried a second formula. No good, the airplane manufacturer claimed. Larsen tried again. And again. And again. Each new mixture was rejected.

Finally, on the fortieth try, Larsen's product was accepted. When the time came to choose a name, Larsen figured WD (water displacement)-40 was ideal.

The lubricant was so effective that workmen at the airport began sneaking small containers of WD-40 home for their own use. Word spread, and soon Rocket Chemical started getting orders for the new product. WD-40 became so popular that eventually Rocket Chemical discontinued its other lines and changed its name to the WD-40 Company. Today it sells nearly $100 million dollars of the miracle lubricant each year.

ANSWERS TO NAME THESE HOME APPLIANCES OR MACHINES:
1. Microwave oven 2. Lawn mower

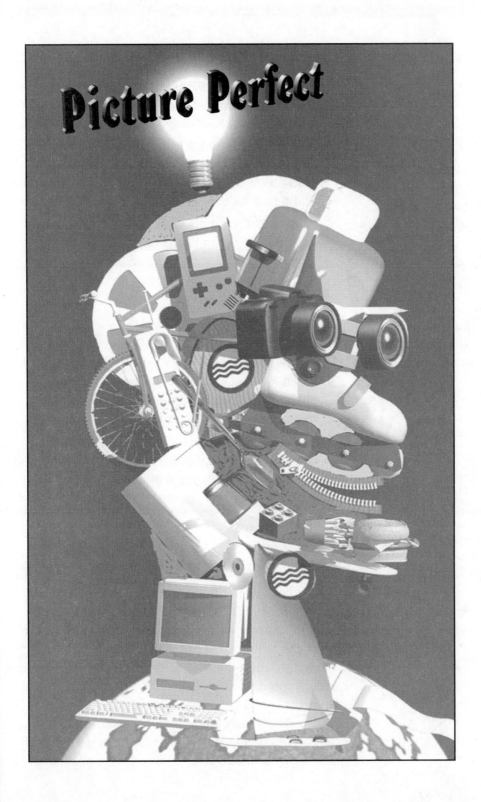

PICTURE PERFECT

Name These Picture-Making, Picture-Taking Inventions:

1. Eadweard Muybridge took thousands of split-second pictures of horses in motion. His fascination with movement led to a new invention and a new form of entertainment.

2. Tired of rewriting documents, Chester Carlson experimented with chemicals, glass slides, and metal plates in his kitchen's apartment until he found a simpler, faster way to do the job.

3. When it was too hot to show home movies indoors, Richard Hollingshead hauled his equipment outside, showed them on the wall of his garage, and created a new film fad.

4. When Edwin Land's daughter wanted to see photographs right away, he did his best. His invention revolutionized the world of photography.

5. Dr. Bela Julez discovered a way of producing computer-generated pictures that seem to leap off the page when you stare at them.

Answers on page 59.

Photography

People have always wanted to make perfect pictures. As far back as the fourth century B.C. the Chinese used something later called the *camera obscura*. In its simplest form the *camera obscura* was a darkened box with a pinhole at one end to let in light. As light passed through the hole, it projected an upside-down image onto the back of the box. To record the picture, an artist traced the image onto paper.

Two Frenchmen, Niecephone Niepce and Louis Daguerre, thought there had to be a better method — some way to make pictures directly, some method of

PHOTO FACTS

In 1835 an English scientist, William Fox Talbot, developed a photographic process that is still used today. He found that by coating paper with a silver compound, then exposing it to light, a negative image developed. From the negative, any number of positive images could be printed.

Other inventors adapted the principles of photography discovered by Talbot and Louis Daguerre and used them in the *camera obscura*. By putting light-sensitive photographic plates at the back of the *camera obscura*, a negative image could be captured, then developed and printed later.

capturing images without having to sketch or paint them.

Niepce was an inventor; Daguerre an artist and stage designer. Together they formed a partnership, shared information and performed experiments. They had limited success with "fixing" an image permanently on a light-sensitive surface. When Niepce died in 1833, Daguerre continued his experiments alone.

One day, after treating a metal sheet with iodine, Daguerre carelessly laid a silver spoon on its surface. When he removed the spoon later, he noticed an odd thing: a faint image of it remained on the metal!

Daguerre immediately recognized what had happened. The silver and iodine had reacted to produce silver iodide. When the iodized silver was exposed to light it darkened, and a hazy image appeared on the metal sheet. Daguerre then treated polished silver plates with iodine and exposed them to light. Sure enough, faint images appeared. Daguerre knew he was on to something. There were two problems, though. The image required a long exposure time, and it soon faded because Daguerre did not know how to fix it permanently on the plate.

Thomas Edison kept notebooks with sketches and notes of his inventions. For the light bulb, he filled 40,000 pages.

One spring day in 1835, after exposing another silver plate to light, Daguerre decided to go to bed early, so he stored the underexposed plate in his chemical cupboard. The next morning when he went to the cupboard to get the plate, he couldn't believe his eyes. On the plate was a picture. Somehow, overnight, a picture had fully developed — on its own.

Daguerre knew that he was close to an important discovery. He suspected something in the cupboard must have developed the image. But which of the many chemicals was it? Each day he deliberately put underexposed plates in the cupboard. Each day he removed one more chemical from the shelves. Still the plates mysteriously continued to develop.

Finally, when there were no more chemicals left in the cupboard, Daguerre again stored a plate in it. By morning an image had appeared. Daguerre was mystified. How could this be? He examined the cupboard closely, and spotted a few drops of spilled mercury in a corner. Mercury vapour! Mercury vapour must have made the images develop!

By using mercury vapour, Daguerre shortened the exposure time. One problem remained, however. The images still darkened after they were developed. But after a few more years of experimenting Daguerre discovered that another chemical, sodium hyposulfate, could "fix" the image on a plate. With that discovery, the picture-making process was complete. Images could be exposed on a light-sensitive surface, developed, then fixed permanently, never to fade again.

Daguerre's discoveries ushered in the age of photography.

3-D IMAGES

3-D Images —
Pictures that Jump Off the Page

They're everywhere, it seems. In Magic Eye books. On greeting cards. On walls and bulletin boards: three-dimensional (3-D) pictures! Stare at one — look *through* the picture rather than *at* it — and a startling image pops out of nowhere.

These effects are called stereograms. To understand how they work, try holding up a finger in front of you. Stare at it, but focus on a faraway object (the back wall, for example).

Close one eye at a time. Look at the finger with the right eye. Then the left. Blink one eye at a time. Does your finger seem to jump from side to side? That's because each eye sees a slightly different image. When your brain processes the images, it fuses them, to produce a single image, one with depth and dimension.

Sir Charles Wheatstone was intrigued by this little trick. He drew two pictures that were almost exactly alike. When he placed them side by side and studied them, the two seemed to join. The result? A single 3-D image!

For a century, inventors experimented with stereograms. In the 1950s they discovered a way of making a printed image produce a 3-D effect. Two images were printed, one in red ink, and on top of that, another in green, creating a blurry picture confusing to the naked eye. To see the image the viewer wears tinted glasses, with one red lens and one green one. Each lens filters out one colour, forcing each eye to see a different picture, either the red one or the green one. The brain rejoins them.

In the 1980s Dr. Bela Julez discovered a way to produce computer-generated stereograms using random dot images. First he generated a square filled with random black or white dots. Then he took the square and shifted a group of dots in it to the side. Where there were gaps because of shifting, Julez filled them with more random dots. Over and over, he repeated the process. When he was finished he had a muddled picture that seemed to be just a sea of dots, but embedded in the dots were sets of similar-looking columns and a hidden image.

When you stare at one of these stereograms, your left eye focuses on the left column of dots. The right eye sees the other. The brain processes the images, interpreting the small differences as depth. At that moment, you recognize something . . . and a picture emerges!

The Kodak Camera

In 1874, at age twenty-four, George Eastman planned to buy a camera and use it to record his first vacation. But the camera was an expensive, heavy device (almost as big as a microwave oven today). To use it he needed other expensive gear: a heavy tripod, bulky photographic glass plates, a dark tent inside which he would spread a sticky light-sensitive jelly on the plates before exposure, chemicals, glass tanks, and other items to develop the pictures. Instructions for the proper use of these materials cost another five dollars.

Eastman soon realized that taking vacation pictures would be *work*. Why couldn't there be a less expensive and simpler system? he wondered. He cancelled his trip and concentrated on improving the complicated picture-taking process. His first task was to find a substitute for the messy jelly that had to be smeared on the glass plates in darkness.

Months of gruelling trial and error followed. Each evening, after a full day at work, Eastman mixed and cooked emulsions in his mother's kitchen. After three years, numerous frustrations and several unsuitable products, he came up with a convenient mix: a layer of light-sensitive flexible celluloid fastened to a paper backing. No more heavy glass plates!

Unfortunately, only a few professional photographers tried out the new film. Most people still shied away from the bulky, expensive camera and accessories. But George Eastman wanted to put photography into everyone's hands. Eventually he developed a simple black box-type camera that anyone could use. The light, flexible film was wound on a spool at the back of the box. To take a picture all you did was aim the camera and press a button to release the shutter. By turning a key outside the box, you advanced the film to the next frame. No more tents, messy chemicals, or heavy equipment to lug around!

In June, 1888, the first of Eastman's cameras went on sale. He named his new cameras Kodak. The name was simple, easy to spell, and easy to remember.

Over the years Eastman improved his camera, making it smaller, lighter, and less expensive. By the time he died in 1932 the heavy, awkward camera of the past had disappeared. A simple, small, light box — much like the one you probably use today — had taken its place.

Celluloid — Miracle Plastic

Celluloid, the material George Eastman used in place of glass plates — has an interesting history of its own. In 1863 ivory, used for making billiard balls, was in short supply. A billiard ball company started a competition, offering a prize to anyone who could find a suitable substitute for ivory. Two New Jersey brothers, Isaiah and John Wesley Hyatt, decided to have a go at it.

One day they were working with a mixture of sawdust, paper, and glue when John accidentally cut his finger. He rushed to the medicine cabinet to get a bottle of collodion. At the time, collodion was often used on cuts because it dried quickly to form an elastic "skin" that sealed the wound. The bottle of collodion had spilled in the cabinet, however, and hardened into a thin clear sheet. That gave John Hyatt an idea. Instead of glue, why not mix collodion with sawdust and paper?

The Hyatt brothers experimented with

collodion and eventually made a material they called celluloid. The first of many plastics, celluloid became the rage and was used in a number of different ways: in collars and cuffs of men's shirts, as knife handles, for dice, buttons, fountain pens, and, of course, as film for cameras.

The Hyatts also made billiard balls from celluloid and entered the contest. They didn't win, however. The celluloid balls tended to shatter on impact, making them unsuitable for the game.

SPOTLIGHT ON INVENTION

Eliminate Parts or Steps to Simplify a Process

Invention is a combination of brains and material. The more brains you use, the less material you need.

— Charles F. Kettering

THE STORY OF THE INSTANT CAMERA

How Less Came to Mean More

Edwin H. Land was on vacation in 1943 when a great idea came to him. He had just snapped a photo of his three-year-old daughter. Like most children, she wanted to see the picture right away. Land patiently explained that she would have to wait until the film came back from the processors. But even as he talked to his daughter, Land was thinking and planning. Was there another way to take pictures? One that didn't take so long for the results to be seen?

Back home, Land tinkered with an idea. In ordinary cameras, once film was exposed it had to be taken out of the camera, then developed, rinsed, washed, dried, and finally printed. Land looked for ways to eliminate several steps, and to have others done inside the camera itself. He started by producing a new kind of film. It consisted of sealed, two-sided packets that contained developing chemicals. Next he invented a camera to use the new film.

With it, once a picture was snapped, a motor advanced a single packet through a set of rollers. The rollers squeezed the packet, breaking it to release the developing chemicals. The chemicals reacted with the film and printed an image on photographic paper in the packet.

No fuss. No mess. No waiting. From start to finish, the process took just sixty seconds.

The first Polaroid Land camera went on sale just before Christmas, 1948. It produced sepia-toned (brownish) prints. The next year Land introduced black-and-white film, and in 1963 colour film became available.

Edwin Land's convenient, no-hassle method of picture taking proved popular with professionals and amateurs alike. Professional photographers liked taking test shots before snapping more polished photographs. Others enjoyed taking, seeing, and having snapshots in an instant.

What do the names Sony, Exxon and Kodak have in common? They were all chosen because the words were easy to say and remember, and did not resemble any particular language.

MORE ABOUT INVENTOR EDWIN LAND

Land saw possibilities in the most ordinary of circumstances. When he was seventeen he was momentarily blinded by the headlights of an oncoming car as he walked down the street. That experience led him to look for some way of reducing glare from light. Six years later, in 1932, he produced a plastic polarizing sheet that filtered light and eliminated glare. He set up a company to manufacture polarizing products. The Polaroid Corporation, producers of non-glare sunglasses and other products, quickly became one of the largest companies in North America, making Edwin Land a wealthy man long before his invention of the instant camera.

Other Simplification-Elimination Inventions
Assembly-Line Mass Production

Henry Ford's earliest automobile, the Model T, was hand-crafted. Each nut and bolt was fastened individually, each coat of paint applied separately. The car was popular, but too expensive for most people to afford. How could he increase production and keep costs down? Ford wondered. He studied the assembly process and realized that it could be made more efficient if some steps were combined or rearranged. Instead of having employees work on one car until it was finished, he had them specialize in one job that they repeated over and over.

Ford rigged up a huge conveyor belt across the factory floor. The moving belt brought parts to workers who stood alongside the belt. Each worker added a piece, tightened a bolt or welded a section. Bit by bit, the car began to take shape as it moved along the belt. By the time it reached the end of the line, the car was fully assembled.

Ford's assembly-line process was such a model of efficiency it was soon adopted by other manufacturers.

Braille At the age of three, Louis Braille was cutting leather in his father's workshop when his knife slipped, cut his face, and blinded him. Louis adapted to his disability, but felt limited because he could not read and write like other children.

Later, when he was fifteen, Louis discovered a system known as "night writing." It had been invented by an army captain so that messages could be sent and read on the battlefield. Night writing used combinations of twelve raised dots that could be felt and "read" with the fingertips.

Louis simplified the system, working out an alphabet that used only six raised dots and adding a series of shortened words and phrases. With Braille it became possible for the blind not only to read messages quickly, but also to write them by using a stylus or typewriter to punch the pattern of dots onto a page.

Zamboni Ice-Resurfacing Machine

Frank Zamboni owned an indoor ice skating rink in California. To keep the ice free of grooves and holes caused by skates, three or four workers had to regularly spend an hour or two resurfacing the ice. To Zamboni this seemed a waste of time and money.

In 1942 he pieced together the first ice-resurfacing machine. It was a primitive-looking device, but it worked. The machine consisted of a huge wooden box on top of a jeep chassis. A conveyor belt scooped ice shavings up and stored them in a compartment, while a fine spray of water built up a new layer of ice behind the machine. With his machine the ice-resurfacing process took minutes instead of hours and could be done by one person instead of three or four. Today Zambonis can be found at sports arenas around the world.

See Also . . .
Scuba Diving (page 120)
Kodak (page 44)

Motion Pictures

A race track in Sacramento, California. Horses thunder down the track, neck and neck. The crowd rises and cheers. A group of men on the sidelines ignore the race. Instead they argue. Some claim that when a horse runs there is a moment when all its feet are off the ground at the same time. The other men say this is impossible. The argument builds and bets are placed. Big bets. To settle the debate the men hire a scientist to study the horse's movements . . .

This scene actually happened in 1877. The scientist hired was Eadweard Muybridge, a man already well known for his study of motion. Muybridge started by setting up forty-eight cameras at regular intervals around the race track. To the shutter of each camera he attached a string that he stretched across the track. As a horse galloped past, the string broke, triggering the shutter to take a picture.

Muybridge now had dozens of pictures, each a few seconds apart from the others. The pictures settled the argument. They showed beyond a shadow of a doubt that there were times when a race horse had all four feet off the ground at once.

Intrigued by the photographs, Muybridge continued his study. He took hundreds of thousands of pictures of all sorts of living things as they moved. His action shots ranged from birds in flight to baseball players running to home plate. The photographs showed motion split seconds apart, but Muybridge still wasn't completely satisfied. He hoped to get them even closer in time.

Muybridge sought help from Thomas Edison, the inventor. Eventually Edison developed the kinetoscope, a large wheel containing hundreds of photographs. To use it a person looked through an opening and cranked a handle to turn the wheel. As each photograph flipped by it was briefly lit by an electric spark. To the viewer, it looked as though the object in the photographs was really moving!

The kinetoscope was the forerunner of our modern motion picture system. Today, when we watch a movie we are really looking at thousands of individual, but closely spaced, pictures that are projected onto a screen so rapidly we don't see them as separate images.

Movie Thrills

The first motion picture was played before a paying audience in a café in Paris on December 28, 1895. Two brothers, Louis and Auguste Lumière, showed ten short films lasting a total of twenty minutes. One of the films featured a steaming train moving toward the audience. The train looked so close and so real that the crowd panicked. Some people even fainted. Since that event, film producers and theatre owners everywhere have looked for new ways to thrill audiences.

MOVIE THRILLS

The Drive-In Movie One summer night in the late 1920s, Richard M. Hollingshead Jr. invited friends over to watch his home movies. It was hot indoors, so Hollingshead moved his equipment outside. He set up his projector on the hood of the family car and used the white wall of his garage as a screen. His guests sat on car seats and lawn furniture.

The event was hit. Neighbours came over to see what was going on, and stayed to watch. They even asked to see the movies a second time.

Being a businessman, Hollingshead saw a money-making opportunity. He found an empty parking lot, erected a huge wooden screen, and on May 6, 1933, opened the world's first drive-in movie theatre.

IMAX The name means "maximum image," and IMAX means just that. Big! Impressive! A movie experience unlike any other.

IMAX was developed by three Canadian movie-makers: Roman Kroitor, Bob Kerr, and Graeme Ferguson. The three wanted to make pictures so clear, large, and spectacular that the viewer became part of them.

Making big pictures seemed simple enough at first. Just start with larger film, then project the image onto a screen that's bigger and farther away than usual. But that's where things became complicated. Most movies are shot on 35-mm film using 35-mm cameras and projectors. For a big screen experience, Kroitor, Kerr, and Ferguson decided to use 70-mm film instead. Unfortunately, existing equipment could not handle the larger film. Because of its size and heavier weight, the film snagged and tore as it passed through ordinary projectors and cameras.

New projectors and cameras had to be invented.

To solve their technical problems, the three film-makers relied on the expertise of others. They sought the help of Bill Shaw, a technician they knew from their high school days. Shaw designed a totally new projection system. Instead of looping the film through upright reels, Shaw used a new invention called the "rolling loop" and ran the film horizontally.

To produce a camera for 70-mm film the film-makers asked a Norwegian inventor, Jan Jacobsen, for help. Four months later Jacobsen had the first IMAX camera ready.

The first IMAX film, *Tiger Child*, aired at Expo '70 in Osaka, Japan. Moviegoers were thrilled by the big-screen experience. Its success paved the way for other IMAX films and the development of new theatres to handle the big-screen picture.

How different is IMAX? Step into an IMAX theatre and you'll notice right away. The screen towers five storeys above you and stretches thirty metres across. The seats are steeply tiered so that no matter where you sit you are never more than fifteen metres from the screen. Your view is clear and unobstructed.

During the show, sound spills from multi-channel speakers placed throughout the theatre. Your body feels the thunder of their vibrations and because the picture is so brilliant, sharp and close, you are engulfed by sounds and images. For a short while you forget where you are. You become part of the action unfolding on the screen.

That's the experience of IMAX — just what its inventors hoped to provide.

Movie Special Effects

Georges Melies, one of France's earliest film producers, was shooting a movie in front of a Paris opera house in 1896 when the film jammed in the camera. Not wanting to stop to fix the problem, Melies continued to shoot the scene. When the film was developed, it revealed an amazing sight. Figures blended together and transformed in the oddest ways: a man changed into a woman, a bus into a hearse.

The accident inspired Melies to experiment with the technique and use it in other films. It also opened up a whole world of possibilities. Other film-makers recognized that the eye could be tricked into believing something was real when it wasn't. Since then special effects have become an important part of movie magic. Since Melies's time, film-makers have experimented with many kinds of special effects. More recently, computers have been used to achieve some spectacular results.

How does the computer help the film-maker? Try a little experiment. Use a magnifying glass to look at a newspaper photograph or drawing. Close up, you can see that the image is not really a blob of colour or a mass of lines. Instead, it is a sea of tightly packed dots. The thousands of dots are so close together that the brain is tricked into believing it sees lines, shapes, and images.

When an image or photograph is programmed into a computer, each of these thousands of dots is remembered as a string of numbers or digits (see Binary Code, page 64). Since the computer is basically a mathematical machine capable of performing operations quickly and easily, once the digits are in its memory they can be manipulated and changed. When that happens, the image changes too.

In 1898 writer H.G. Wells described a laser-like heat ray in his novel, The War of the Worlds. The real laser beam was invented in 1958.

With the computer, digital images can be created, coloured, textured, combined, stretched, reduced, rotated, and repeated. In short, the computer gives the film-maker new tricks to stun and amaze audiences.

Mix, Match, Blend, and Combine: Compositing

In *Star Wars*, Luke Skywalker and Darth Vadar battle it out with light sabres inside a huge spaceship while the crew works at stations in the background. Behind, through a giant window, we see glittering stars and approaching spacecraft.

Most of this scene is pure movie magic, the result of a process known as compositing. In *Star Wars*, as in many other films, various elements of a scene were filmed separately. The actors portraying Luke Skywalker and Darth Vadar worked through their battle sequence on a sound stage. The scene of the crew at work was filmed on another set. Animation experts used models and paintings to create the star field and approaching starships. Once the separate scenes were ready, a computer was used to composite the images. The film clips and sound effects were digitized, then combined and blended into one to complete the illusion.

Transform One Thing Into Another: Morphing

Television commercials or movies often show one object or person changing into another. A car becomes a tiger. A robot becomes a person. The transformation happens so quickly and smoothly that the viewer can not tell how it was done. Most likely a computer technique called morphing was used to achieve the result.

In morphing the computer compares the dot arrangement of the starting image (the car, for example) and the after-image (the tiger). The computer looks for similarities between the two, and averages together the dots that make certain features. With the help of the programmer, the computer sets up a series of shifts and relocations so that dots from one image move or dissolve into the other.

Create New Worlds: Fractal Generation

Many natural objects such as rivers, waterfalls, coastline, plants, and mountain ranges are composed of repeated smaller shapes or fractals. From a distance, for example, a mountain looks like a giant triangle. Seen more closely, the peaks, ridges, and valleys look like triangle shapes, too, although they might be set at different angles and joined in random ways.

Once a computer is programmed to draw the smallest of these shapes, it can be instructed to repeat the shape as many times as necessary. To construct a mountain, for example, the computer is given the basic triangle shape. The computer generates other triangles, sometimes joining one to the other, other times inserting small ones inside larger ones until the framework of an entire mountain has been created. Once a "skin" (colour and texture) is added to the framework, a convincing mountain exists on the screen.

Through fractal generation, the film-maker can create new worlds without the use of expensive props and scenery.

Make the Imaginary Come Alive: Computer Animation

In *Jurassic Park*, dinosaurs stomp across the screen. Monkeys, rhinos, and elephants create havoc in *Jumanji*. And in *Dragonheart*, the world's last dragon swoops and roars. The creatures in these movies never stormed a sound stage, of course. Most were

In 1952 Orville Redenbacker and a friend, Charles Bowan, teamed up to produce a new hybrid popping corn that popped fluffier than other varieties.

products of computer animation.

If you look at a piece of movie film, you can see that it is actually a sequence of still pictures, each one slightly different from the next. The pictures move so quickly that the eye is tricked into believing it sees motion.

In traditional animation each picture is drawn and coloured individually. Since it takes twenty-four separate frames to produce one second of film, a fifteen-minute cartoon might require over 30,000 individually drawn pictures.

With the computer, new animation techniques are available. By using a process known as "in-betweening," for example, the tedious drawing method can be simplified. The animator starts by entering two or more key frames of a segment of film into the computer. Then the artist supplies enough information so that the computer can complete the action by drawing the pictures that fit between the key frames.

With the computer, the animator can also draw directly on the screen. For *Toy Story*, animators created digitized characters and scenes and used the computer to alter the movements in each frame to give the illusion of motion.

To make computer-generated creatures like the dinosaurs in *Jurassic Park* or the dragon in *Dragonheart*, animators often start with a clay model. Once they are satisfied with its appearance, they generate a wire-frame skeleton of the creature on the computer screen. By programming the computer with instructions for movement, animators move the wire-frame model through a sequence of changes. In the final stages, colour, shading, and texture are added to give the creature its realistic appearance.

Photocopier

Chester F. Carlson's hand hurt. His eyes, too. As a patent analyzer he faced long hours of writing and drawing every day, recopying and redrawing from clients' originals, making sure that each fact and every sketch was the same. For a man who was nearsighted and arthritic, this was painful.

In the 1930s there was only one other way to do the task: photograph the original, then develop the negative in chemical baths, enlarge and print it. The process was messy and took hours, sometimes days, to produce decent results.

Figuring there had to be some way to make a "dry" instant copy, Carlson spent his evenings at the New York Public Library, reading every item about photography and copying he could find. He found an article by a Hungarian scientist that described how charged particles attached themselves to oppositely charged surfaces. The article got Carlson thinking.

Working from his apartment kitchen, he conducted experiments in static electricity and photography. He tinkered with glass slides, metal plates, and assorted chemicals. The big break came on October 22, 1938. Carlson wrote the date and the word "Astoria" (the suburb of New York where he lived) on a glass microscope slide. With a handkerchief he rubbed a sulphur-coated metal plate to give it an electrical charge, then attached the glass slide to the metal plate, exposed both to bright light, and separated the pieces. Next he sprinkled powder on the metal plate and pressed it to a sheet of paper. A clear copy of "10-22-38 ASTORIA" appeared. The paper was heated to "fix" the image, making it permanent and smudge-free.

Knowing that his idea could work, Carlson now tried to construct a machine that would do the job. But that took money, something Carlson no longer had. Figuring that businesses might be interested in

PHOTOCOPIER FACTS

Carlson's dry copy process was called *xerography*. The name comes from the Greek: *xeros* means "dry" and *graphos* means "writing."

IBM, GE, and RCA are among the businesses that initially turned down Chester Carlson's invention.

Almost everyone who invested in Carlson's invention profited in a big way. One man started with a $1000 investment in the Haloid Company. Eventually, his stock became worth over $1.5 million.

Xerox did well too. In 1959, the year the copy machine was introduced, Haloid's profits were $2 million. By 1963 profits had leaped to $22 million. Today Xerox is a multi-billion-dollar company.

his invention, he approached different companies, but most laughed at the idea. An interesting concept, they said, but too expensive and impractical. For five years Carlson visited one company after another. Tired and discouraged, he almost abandoned his project, until a small company in Rochester, New York, decided to gamble on his dry copier. The Haloid Company, maker of photographic papers, took what little money it had in reserve and bought a license to develop a copying machine based on Carlson's design. It took years to work out the bugs and make the idea practical, but the gamble paid off. In 1959, almost twenty-five years after Carlson started his experiments, Haloid introduced the 914 copier, the first fully automated dry copy machine to use ordinary paper.

The machine was a huge success. Eventually, Haloid changed its name to the Xerox Corporation, which is one of the largest and most successful companies in North America today. Chester Carlson became extremely wealthy, too. With his royalties, he made millions. By the time he died in 1968 he had donated much of his fortune to charity.

ANSWERS TO NAME THESE PICTURE-MAKING, PICTURE-TAKING INVENTIONS:
1. Film projector and motion pictures 2. Photocopying 3. Drive-in movies
4. Polaroid instant camera 5. Computer-generated 3-D pictures or stereograms

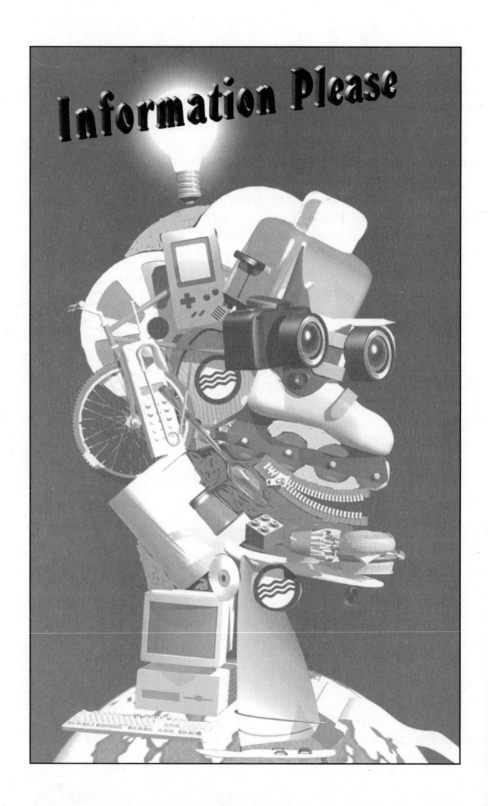

INFORMATION PLEASE

Name These Hi-Tech Devices:

1. Although his invention filled a room, used dozens of switches and levers, and never worked, Charles Babbage is honoured as the father of the tool we use to travel the information highway.

2. John Baird assembled the first of these with odds-and-ends such as an old motor from an electric fan, an empty biscuit box, darning needles, and spare radio parts. Today many people have one, two, or more of these around the home.

3. The first of these "facsimile" machines was invented by an Italian priest years before there were telephones, or even light bulbs.

4. By combining two different inventions, earphones and a small tape player, Sony produced one of the most popular inventions of the past two decades.

5. The words "Mr. Watson, come here. I want you!" proved that this invention was a success.

ANSWERS on page 82.

Our alphabet was invented by the Phoenicians 5,000 years ago.

Computer

The computer has been an invention in the making for over 200 years. No one person invented it, but one name from the past stands above the rest: Charles Babbage.

Babbage was an English inventor and mathematician who lived in the 1800s. In his day people from many walks of life used complicated mathematical tables to plan for the future. Bankers used charts to calculate interest rates; astronomers used them to plot the movements of planets; ship captains relied on navigational charts to set their course across the ocean. Data in the charts was computed by hand using long formulas that filled pages. Small mistakes were easy to make, and sometimes these led to bigger ones.

One evening in 1812, when Babbage was just twenty-one years old, an idea came to him as he used these mathematical tables. A machine could do the job! A machine could calculate faster and more accurately than any human.

Babbage set out to make such a machine. In 1822 he built a mechanical calculator known as the difference engine. The difference engine performed simple calculations involving up to eight decimal places. It was an improvement over other calculating systems of his day, but Babbage wasn't satisfied. He wanted a faster machine, one that could automatically repeat calculations, store numbers, even print the results.

Babbage drew detailed plans for a steam-driven machine he called the analytical engine. The new machine was to be immense and complicated, a maze of cylinders, wheels, levers, rods, and springs. It would work this way: Columns of wheels inside the machine stored numbers. Instructions were fed into the machine on punched cards. The pattern of holes on the cards represented numbers and operations. The cards triggered levers and gears, turned wheels, and enabled the machine to perform the calculations punched on the cards. The analytical engine had other features, too. It had a memory for storing information, and a built-in printer to reproduce the results.

In 1832 Babbage started work on his computing machine. He ran into numerous problems. As he refined his ideas he redrew his plans, forcing his workers to abandon what they were doing and start over again. When his frustrated financial backers withdrew their support he dipped into his own funds to cover his costs. Worse yet, he faced ridicule by other mathematicians who thought his ideas were foolish, even dangerous. For thirty-seven years, Babbage toiled over the analytical engine, convinced he could make it work. He never did.

Babbage's ideas were sound, but ahead of their time. His plans called for delicate machinery to run the engine, finely tuned parts that required great accuracy — something not technically possible in his day. But Babbage had a vision of the future that few others did. The analytical engine had all the essential parts of a modern computer: an input or programming system, a central processing unit, a memory, and a printer.

A hundred years later, modern electronics made possible what Babbage in his time could not. With switches, circuits, and electrical energy taking the place of wheels, levers, and gears, the digital computer became a reality.

The world's first ATM (automated teller machine) was installed in London, England, in 1967.

MORE ABOUT INVENTOR CHARLES BABBAGE

Charles Babbage invented other useful things, among them a cowcatcher (the grill at the front of train engines), a machine for recording earthquake waves, a skeleton key, a speedometer, and the ophthalmoscope, an instrument used by doctors to see inside the eye.

Babbage's friend and fellow mathematician, Lady Augusta Ada Lovelace, supported his ideas. She promoted the analytical engine and even wrote its first programs, making her the world's first computer programmer. A computer language has been named "Ada" in her honour.

In 1911, forty years after Babbage's death, his son actually built part of the analytical engine to prove that his father's ideas would have worked.

More About Computers
Binary Code: The Language

of Computers The number language computers use and understand was developed in the 1800s by George Boole, a British mathematician.

The binary code uses combinations of only two numbers — 0 and 1. The 0s and 1s in the code trigger electrical impulses inside the computer. A one (1) opens a switch and sends an electrical pulse along wires. A zero (0) closes a switch and shuts down the electrical impulse. Each letter, symbol, number, or line keyed into the computer is changed into strings of 0s and 1s. When, for example, a 5 is entered, the computer translates it into binary language as 101 (open-close-open). The letter *a* in binary code is 01000001. Every keyboard or mouse entry has its own series of binary code numbers that instruct the computer to open and close switches at lightning speed.

Binary digits, or bits, can be stored as magnetized dots on a disk or hard drive. Bits can also be stored as tiny pits along spiral tracks on a compact disk.

Computer Update The first digital computers were bulky affairs, weighing tonnes, containing thousands of electronic tubes, and occupying the space of several rooms. Several other inventions helped downsize the computer, making it today's handy desktop machine.

In 1943 Paul Eisler, a German engineer, patented the first printed circuit board. With his method, miniature circuits could be printed on copper foil attached to plastic boards. The printed circuit board replaced complicated and cumbersome wiring in the computer.

In 1947 three Americans, William Schockley, John Bardeen, and Walter Brattain, invented the transistor. Transistors detect and amplify current, as well as open and close circuits. Tiny transistors replaced the large electronic tubes used in the earliest computers.

American Jack Kilby invented the microchip or integrated circuit in 1958. In the microchip, miniaturized electronic components are embedded in a thin layer of semiconductor material such as silicon. With microchips, entire circuits and functions can be squeezed into a very small space.

Japanese inventor Yoshiro Nakamats invented the floppy disk in 1950. It contains a flexible magnetic sheet which stores electrical impulses from the computer as patterns of magnetism. With the floppy, lengthy programs and data can be saved, retrieved, and transported, all on the same thin sheet. Today computers use hard drives for even greater memory capacity. They contain several hard magnetic disks sandwiched together and enclosed, to keep them dust-free.

The mouse was designed in 1965 by American inventor Douglas Englebart, but it was not used in home computers until 1983. As the sphere on the mouse's underside slides on a mat or desk top, it sends electrical impulses that inform the computer of its position. A click of the mouse turns on a switch, to which the computer responds by completing a command.

The Internet Surf the Net. Join the World Wide Web. Talk to other computers around the globe . . .

The Internet had its beginnings almost thirty years ago, not for the purposes of chat, but for defence. In 1969 the United States military had computers at several bases across the country. They were linked in a chain, one computer to another to the next. The problem, the military realized, was that if one computer was disabled because of an attack, the others would be affected too. With the chain of communication broken, one base would not be able to communicate with another, and vital information might be lost. This was a serious security risk. What if, they reasoned, the computers were networked instead: linked not in a chain, but in a web, with each in touch with all other computers. That way, if one computer failed, others in the web could still communicate. So the Department of Defense created ARPANET (ARPA stands for Advanced Research Projects Administration), a network of computer links, three in California and one in Utah. The designers of the system figured ARPANET had limited use (one person called it "one of the biggest bloopers ever"). But ARPANET was a wild success.

People at universities figured that networking was the perfect way to share research and information, so they started their own system. Large companies realized the advantages and got on board to create other systems. Each network interlinked with the others, making the large global system we now call the Internet.

FAX Machine

All across Florence, Italy, tongues wagged. Giovanni Caselli's neighbours called him an oddball. Some people even wondered if he had sold his soul to the devil.

Caselli was a nineteenth-century priest who dabbled in science. He read all the scientific journals he could find, and even converted his small home into a cluttered laboratory where he conducted experiments on his own.

The telegraph was one of the new inventions of his day. With it, messages could be sent quickly over long distances from one telegraph station to another, using a system of clicks and clacks known as Morse code. The telegraph changed the world of communication, but Caselli realized that there were limitations to its use. Only one message could be sent over a single wire at any one time, and documents never actually changed hands. The original message had to be coded at one end, then decoded at the other. It took specially trained operators to do that.

Caselli set out to improve the telegraph. With the help of another technician, Caselli toiled in his makeshift laboratory. He rigged up a model telegraph system, added batteries, coils of wire, parts of clocks, even pendulums. For seven years he fine-tuned his device. All the while he put up with ridicule from others who thought he was crazy. Finally, in 1863, Caselli unveiled his invention.

The pantelegraph, as he called it, looked odd. It stood almost two metres tall and was shaped somewhat like a grand piano set on end. It had two sides, one for transmitting messages, the other for receiving them from another pantelegraph. Pendulums hung at either end. Clocks kept the swinging pendulums synchronized while batteries powered the device.

FAX FACTS

Caselli's FAX machine appeared before the telephone (1876) or light bulb (1879).

Modern FAX machines use computer technology that changes pictures and messages into digital signals. The signals are sent over existing telephone wires to a receiving machine, which decodes the signals and prints the message.

To transmit a message, the sender first wrote with ink on a metal plate. The plate was then placed under the pendulum at the transmitting end of the pantelegraph. The pendulum's metal tip swung over the plate and made contact with the surface. When it struck an uninked section it completed an electrical circuit that sent power to a second pendulum on another pantelegraph. The receiving pendulum swung over chemically treated paper. With each electrical impulse it discoloured the paper, leaving an exact image of the original message.

With Caselli's clever device, complicated codes could be forgotten. The receiver obtained an actual copy, or facsimile, of the sender's message. The pantelegraph reproduced handwritten notes, printed messages, even drawings and pictures. Several messages could be sent over a single wire at the same time, too.

Caselli's invention became the world's first practical FAX (facsimile) machine. The French government quickly capitalized on the revolutionary device. Using existing telegraph wires it set up a FAX line between Paris and the city of Lyon. At top speed, the pantelegraph transmitted forty messages in a single hour. Impressed with its abilities, the French government opened other lines and added other pantelegraphs.

When war broke out in 1870, the FAX service was interrupted. After the war, the system was abandoned. Perhaps it was too expensive. Perhaps the invention was too advanced for its time. Whatever the reasons, Caselli's pantelegraph disappeared. By the time FAX machines reappeared decades later, technology had changed so much that small, portable machines could replace the cumbersome, heavy pantelegraph.

Radio

When he was a teenager Guglielmo Marconi rigged up a laboratory in the attic of his parents' home in northern Italy. His father was not pleased.

In school, Marconi often did poorly. He failed exams. He was in constant trouble with teachers. His father figured Marconi needed an iron hand and strict rules. Marconi thought otherwise. He wanted to be a scientist, inventor, or engineer. He read every scientific article he could find, and even though he could not pass the exams needed to enter university, he knew more about electricity and magnetism than many professors.

Marconi was fascinated by the work of a German scientist, Heimrich Hertz. Hertz had discovered that invisible waves of energy travelled through the air whenever electricity sparked across a gap. Marconi was quick to realize the importance of such a discovery. Find some way to harness the waves, he reasoned, and signals might be sent through the air over long distances without ever needing connecting wires or cables.

Despite his father's objections, Marconi started work in his attic laboratory. Using equipment he made himself, and other supplies he borrowed from a nearby university, he built a primitive transmitter. He set up a terminal at one side of the attic, then rigged up a bell and a second terminal at the other side.

In 1895, after months of effort and many failed attempts, Marconi did what many others considered impossible. He sent a signal across his attic that rang a bell. Excited by this success, he looked at ways to increase the distance the waves travelled. He took his equipment outdoors and sent a signal across the

RADIO FACTS

The first voice transmission was made on December 23, 1900, by Canadian Reginald A. Fessenden. Fessenden's message: "Is it snowing where you are, Mr. Thiessen?" Distance transmitted: 1.5 kilometres.

The first radio program was also Fessenden's. On Christmas Eve, 1906, he broadcast two musical tunes, a poem and a short announcement to ships in the Caribbean from a transmitting station in Massachusetts. ➡

yard. When he tried sending signals farther, though, he couldn't. They were too weak.

One day as he experimented outdoors, Marconi left one of his terminals on a small hill. Suddenly the signal became stronger. Working on a hunch, he placed his receiving terminal high atop a metal pole. Then he attached a wire to the transmitter and sunk it deep into the ground. With this arrangement he found he could send signals farther than ever.

By the middle of 1895 Marconi was astounding the scientific world by sending signals well over a kilometre. Even his father was impressed. But Marconi was just beginning.

Through experiments he discovered ways of increasing the strength of his signals and the distance they travelled. He found that metal sheets around the antennae channelled the waves into concentrated beams. He also found that he could send signals farther by stringing antennae into long-distance chains, then relaying messages from one antenna to another. By 1899 Marconi succeeded in sending a signal across the English Channel, a distance of over forty-three kilometres, but still he was not satisfied. He had his sights set on sending signals across something even wider — the Atlantic Ocean.

In 1900 he constructed his largest and most powerful transmitter yet on the coast of England. On the other side of the ocean, in St. John's, Newfoundland, he built a receiver. To get the receiver high enough to capture signals, Marconi attached it to a kite. On December 11, 1901, he launched the receiver high into the air. From England, a friend tapped out a message in Morse code. Across an ocean more than 3000 kilometres wide, Marconi received the message, proving to the world that long-distance wireless communication was indeed possible.

RADIO FACTS

The portable radio was invented by J. McWilliams Stone of Chicago in 1922. Called the Operadio, it weighed about nine kilograms and cost $180.

George Frost, an eighteen-year-old American, created the first car radio. He installed it in a Model T Ford in 1922.

In 1955 Sony produced the TR-55, the world's first transistor radio.

Sound Systems

Today we have sophisticated systems capable of turning out high-quality sound, but the whole thing started with a vibrating needle, a bleeding finger, and a very curious inventor.

In 1877 Thomas Edison, inventor of the light bulb and holder of a thousand other patents, studied the telephone, a new invention in his day. He hoped to improve its performance, so he took apart the receiver to take a closer look.

When he spoke into it he noticed that the diaphragm, a thin sheet, vibrated. How strong were the vibrations? he wondered. To find out, he attached a steel needle to the diaphragm. Now when he spoke he could see the needle bounce. He could feel the vibrations, too, by touching the needle with his finger. The vibrations were strong, the needle sharper than expected. When Edison touched it, he pricked his finger.

Most people would have patched up the wound and continued with their work, but Edison was struck by the oddity of the accident. Suddenly he had an idea. If sound could cause a needle to vibrate, then maybe the shaking needle could etch lines into a soft material. Perhaps another needle passing over these marks could then cause the sound to be repeated.

Edison held a piece of heavy paper near the needle and spoke into the telephone again. When he passed the pricked paper back a second time, the needle followed the marks it had made, and Edison heard his own voice faintly repeated. He had the beginnings of a sound-recording system.

Inspired by the incident, Edison went on to invent a "talking machine." It was a copper cylinder, covered with tin foil, that was turned by hand. On

Thomas Edison holds the record for the greatest number of patents: 1093.

December 6, 1877, Edison tested his invention. He recited "Mary Had a Little Lamb" into a horn attached to the machine. As he spoke, a needle vibrated and cut lines into the tin foil. When Edison passed the needle over the same lines a second time, he heard a scratchy recording of his own voice.

Edison was delighted! So were thousands of others. The "talking machine" or phonograph opened up a whole new world of listening and recording possibilities.

MORE ABOUT INVENTOR THOMAS EDISON

When he was barely twenty, Edison invented the ticker tape machine, a device that told brokers the prices of stocks on the New York Stock Exchange. This invention sold so well that he was able to quit his regular job and devote all of his time to inventing.

Ideas for new inventions seemed to leap out of Edison's mind. Often he saw possibilities in situations other people ignored. He jotted notes and sketches in notebooks, and worked on several ideas at one time.

Edison never needed much rest. He worked around the clock and kept a cot in his laboratory for short naps during the day.

Famous Edison quotations:

Genius is one percent inspiration and ninety-nine percent perspiration.

Everything comes to him who hustles while he waits.

Sound Improvements Edison's talking machine started a revolution in sound. Before long, electricity replaced the hand-operated crank, and flat plastic discs — phonograph records — replaced the copper cylinder and tin foil. Later, amplifiers and speakers were added to improve sound quality. Today, phonographs and records have all but disappeared, and "talking machines" are nothing like Edison's. In their place, we have new and more advanced ways to record and play back sound.

Tape Recorders and Answering Machines
Valdemar Poulsen worked as a technician for the Copenhagen Telephone Company. Each day he watched telephone operators at work, answering telephones, taking messages, redirecting calls. Wouldn't it be easier if a machine recorded messages, then played them back later? he asked himself.

Poulsen recalled several school experiments. In one, iron shavings or filings were sprinkled near a magnet. Tugged by the magnetic field, the iron filings arranged themselves into arc-shaped patterns around the magnet. Similar patterns were produced when filings were sprinkled near electrical wires, proving that electricity produced magnetic fields too. Electricity? Magnetic fields? The two were obviously related. Was there some connection to sound, as well? Poulsen wondered.

In a telephone transmitter, sound changed into electrical impulses that ran along a wire. In the receiver, the electrical impulses were changed back into sound. Poulsen thought that perhaps he could go one step further, and find some way of changing electrical impulses into magnetic patterns and saving them on wire or metal strips. Later, the stored patterns could be converted into electrical impulses and then back into sound again.

Poulsen read about the work of other inventors who had already tested some of these ideas. Then, in 1898, he began work on a recording machine. His machine ran a magnetized steel wire between two spinning spools. When someone spoke into the machine, the voice created electrical impulses that changed the magnetic patterns in the steel wire. When the wire was run back through the machine, the magnetic patterns were converted into electrical impulses, then into sound, enabling the voice to be heard again.

Poulsen called his invention the telegraphone. It was the world's first answering machine, but because of its bulky size and poor sound quality it never gained popularity. Poulsen's invention did prove, however, that magnetic recording was possible. Other inventors followed his lead, made improvements to the machine, and developed the efficient tape recording machines we use today.

Magnetic Tape In 1928, magnetic recording tape, another of Poulsen's ideas, replaced the steel wire in the recording machine. The paper or plastic tape, coated with magnetic powder, was lighter, more flexible, and allowed multiple tracks to be recorded at the same time.

A form of Poulsen's steel wire recorder is still used today. Aircraft carry flight recorders, or black boxes, that use wire in place of tape because it is more durable.

Video recorders use magnetic tape too. Video as well as sound signals are stored as magnetic patterns. The first video recorder, built in 1956, was the size of a piano and used tape that was two inches (about five centimetres) wide.

Compact Disc Players Like many modern inventions, the compact disc (CD) player was the result of many scientists and inventors working together, each building on the ideas of the other. One of these scientists was Theodore Maiman, who invented the first practical laser in 1960.

Maiman had read about Charles Townes, a physicist who came up with a way of amplifying microwaves. Could light be amplified in a similar way? Maiman wondered. He started with a rod of ruby. Both ends of the rod were highly polished and coated with silver so that they acted as mirrors. Maiman flooded the rod with high intensity light. The light bounced back and forth, reflected by the mirrored ends. As it bounced, the light built in intensity until it was strong enough to escape from one end of the rod as a powerful red beam — a laser.

At first people were uncertain how to use the laser. Then, within months of Maiman's discovery, laser fever spread. Inventors took advantage of it and used lasers in new devices.

The CD player is based on laser technology. A compact disc is a digital recording of sound. In a digital recording, the sound signal is converted into a binary code (see page 64). The code is hidden in narrow spiral tracks on the CD. When the CD is played, it rotates at high speeds. A laser beam reads the code and converts it back to sound.

SPOTLIGHT ON INVENTION

Combine Two Products to Make a New One

Great discoveries and improvements invariably involve the cooperation of many minds.

— Alexander Graham Bell

The best way to have a good idea is to have lots of ideas.

— Linus Pauling

THE STORY OF THE WALKMAN

How 1 + 1 Equalled a New 1

Masaru Ibuka often roamed the halls of the Sony Corporation. After all, he was the honorary chairman of the company and he liked to keep on top of new developments. One day in 1978 Ibuka poked his head into one room to watch a team of engineers at work. They were making new headphones, the lightest, most portable set ever produced by Sony. Ibuka was impressed. Small as they were, the headphones gave an amazingly clear and crisp sound.

Later Ibuka visited another department. He heard music coming from a cassette tape player on a nearby desk. Again he was impressed. The player was smaller than any he had seen before, but its sound quality was excellent.

When Ibuka asked an engineer about the machine, he was told that it was a failed invention. The engineering team had been trying to make a portable stereo tape recorder. They managed to squeeze two tiny speakers and a playback unit into a small box, but there was no room to fit a recording device. Figuring that no one would want an invention that only played cassette tapes, but couldn't record on them, the engineers abandoned the project. They just kept the machine around the shop to play music.

Ibuka suddenly remembered the lightweight headphones he had seen earlier on the other side of the building. Why not use them in place of the speakers? That way its sound would improve, the whole unit would be lighter, and because it took less power to run, batteries would last longer too.

Not everyone in the company agreed with Ibuka's brainwave. Who would want to use headphones when they could have speakers? Who would want a tape recorder that didn't record?

Ibuka was an influential person, however, and production on the invention soon started. Dubbed the Walkman, the new player surprised everyone. People loved it. It was small enough to fit in a pocket or briefcase, light enough to hold in the hand while jogging or walking, and its sound quality was remarkable.

Other Combination Inventions

Alka-Seltzer A.H. Beardsley, the president of a chemical company, visited the editor of a newspaper in Indiana in December of 1928. A wave of colds and flu had swept the nation, keeping many people at home and away from work. Not one person at the newspaper was affected, however.

Amazed, Beardsley asked how that was possible. The editor told him about a simple concoction his staff used when they felt a cold coming on. First they took a tablet or two of aspirin. Then they mixed bicarbonate of soda in water and drank the mixture.

When he got back to his lab Beardsley instructed his chemists to make a

Today there are 5.75 million telephone lines in use around the world.

Alexander Graham Bell thought telephones should be answered with the words "Hoy, hoy!" Inventor Thomas Edison suggested something simpler. Just say "Hello," he advised.

Originally, only operators could make connections between parties on the telephone. That came to an end in 1891. Almon B. Strowger, a funeral director from Kansas City, suspected that telephone operators were being paid by his rivals to redirect his calls and steal business. He took out a patent on a "girl-less, cuss-less, out-of-order-less, wait-less" telephone. In his desire to do away with operators, he invented the world's first phone for callers to make their own connections. ➡

tablet that contained both aspirin and bicarbonate of soda. The new medication was called Alka-Seltzer.

Kraft Dinner During the 1930s, the Kraft company tried selling packages of low-priced cheddar cheese powder. No one wanted them. Left with cases of the stuff, one salesman tied packages of cheese powder to boxes of macaroni and started selling the two together. He called the new item Kraft Dinner. People loved the convenience and taste of the product, and before long Kraft made the cheesy noodles an official part of their line.

See Also . . .
Ice Cream Bar (page 16)
Mountain Bike (page 115)
Windsurfer (page 125)

Telephone

In the 1870s the telegraph was the most efficient and fast way to send a message over a long distance. Unfortunately, only a single message could be sent along a telegraph wire at any one time. Two men, Alexander Graham Bell, an inventor and teacher of the deaf, and his assistant, Thomas Watson, aimed to change that. Working from a cramped attic laboratory, they worked at a tangle of springs, reeds and electromagnets trying to find some way to send several messages at once along a single wire.

On the afternoon of June 2, 1875, the situation seemed hopeless. At one end of the attic where they worked Watson tapped the keys of his telegraph transmitter. Across the attic, in another room, Bell pressed his ear to the receiver, tuning each reed one by one. Suddenly there was an accident. One of

Watson's transmitter springs jammed. He snapped at the spring, trying to set it free. Again and again he plucked the spring.

In the other room, Bell bent low, listening to the reeds as he adjusted them. All at once he heard a faint musical hum from one of his receiver reeds. Bell raced from the room shouting, "What did you do? Don't touch anything! Let me see!" Watson showed him that the spring on the transmitter had stuck, and how he had tried to pluck it loose. Bell ordered him to keep plucking while he returned to his room and pressed his ear against the receiver.

Again Bell heard the hum. To his sensitive ear the sound was exactly the same pitch and loudness as Watson's plucked spring. The mishap showed Bell that a sound could be sent over wire and duplicated exactly in a receiver. Over the next months, Bell and Watson worked at improving their device.

Finally, on the morning of Friday, March 10, 1876, Bell spoke into a mouthpiece. At the other end of the line, several rooms away, Watson heard the muffled message in his receiver: "Mr. Watson, come here. I want you!" Thomas Watson rushed to Bell and repeated his message.

Instead of a cumbersome series of clicks and clacks, the two men had succeeded in transmitting far more: the human voice!

TELEPHONE FACTS

An emergency drove William Gray to invent a new telephone convenience. One night in 1887 his wife became very ill. Gray searched for a telephone to call a doctor. He begged permission at a nearby factory, but was refused. After much searching, he located a phone and made the necessary call. The experience so haunted Gray that he invented the first pay telephone.

The modern cellular telephone was first used in the 1970s. In the cellular system, regions or areas are divided into small "cells," each with its own antenna. When a call is made from a cell phone, the electrical signal is converted into a radio signal. The radio signal is transmitted to an antenna in the nearest cell, then relayed to other cells. A computer automatically monitors the frequency and controls the passage of the signal.

Television

Who invented television? A difficult question. Difficult because, as with many complex inventions, no one person takes all the credit. In the case of the tube, dozens of people working oceans apart over the past century helped make television what it is today.

One of the key players was an out-of-work Scottish engineer, John Logie Baird. Not that Baird wanted a steady job, or even tried to find one; he was much too busy for that. Dreaming up new inventions came easily to him and he spent his time tinkering in his workshop. None of his ideas was practical or popular, however, and by the time he was thirty-four he was penniless and frustrated.

One day in 1923 he went for a walk. As he walked he thought about a new invention of his day, radio. If sound could be transmitted by electronic means, why not pictures? he wondered. By the time he returned home, Baird had a plan.

He gathered a bunch of odds-and-ends: an old motor from an electric fan, an empty biscuit box, darning needles, a tea chest, a lens from a bicycle light, and spare radio parts. Working in his cramped quarters he assembled the bits and pieces.

The tea chest formed the base of his contraption. To this he attached the motor. Cardboard cut-outs (used as scanning disks) were mounted on darning needles that were fixed to the motor. The biscuit tin held a lamp. The whole thing was fastened together with glue, string, and sealing wax.

Baird spent months fiddling with the flimsy device. Finally, one afternoon in February, 1924, he successfully transmitted a flickering image of a cross onto a white sheet behind the contraption. Excited by these results, he borrowed money from relatives and worked part time as a shoe shiner and razor blade

Thomas Edison's first successful light bulb glowed for forty hours, starting on October 19, 1879.

salesman to raise extra cash. He moved into a stuffy attic workshop in London and continued his experiments.

His greatest breakthrough came on October 2, 1925, when he transmitted the image of a ventriloquist's dummy from one end of the attic to the other. Thrilled, he ran downstairs to the office below, nabbed a young worker named William Taynton, and convinced him to become the first human television star.

"I placed him before the transmitter," Baird wrote later, "and went into the next room to see what the screen would show. The screen was entirely blank. Puzzled and disappointed I went back to the transmitter, and there the cause of the failure became evident. The boy, scared by the strong light, had backed away from the transmitter. I gave him some money, and this time he kept his head in the right position. Going again into the next room, I saw his head on the screen quite clearly. It is amusing that the first person in the world to be seen by television needed to be bribed to accept that distinction!"

Overnight, Baird became famous. He set up demonstrations of his invention, and received financial help from wealthy sponsors to continue his work. In 1929 the British Broadcasting Corporation used Baird's system to make its first television broadcast, and for a time he even had his own nightly television show.

But the success did not last. Other inventors

TELEVISION FACTS

Baird's first televised picture was nothing like those seen today. It was bright pink with stripes. Because it flashed only ten times a second, the picture flickered and was difficult to watch.

Two Americans, Philo T. Farnsworth and Vladimir Zworykin, worked independently to invent systems that converted images electronically. The electronic systems had fewer lines, greater range, and transmitted images more clearly than Baird's mechanical method. ➡

81

devised better ways of transmitting pictures. Unable and unwilling to adapt to change, Baird moved on to other projects.

John Logie Baird died in 1946 at the age of fifty-eight, still bitter and disappointed about the treatment his invention had received.

ANSWERS TO NAME THESE HI-TECH DEVICES:
1. Computer 2. Television 3. FAX machine 4. Walkman 5. Telephone

TELEVISION FACTS

Television (and motion pictures) work because of a principle known as persistence of vision. The human eye is slower than the brain. If single images are sent rapidly, the brain blurs them together, creating the illusion of a smoothly moving picture.

Television didn't take long to catch on. By 1931 there were an estimated 30,000 television sets in the United States alone. Today there are nearly 100 million. And on a typical day, Canadians buy 3836 colour TVs.

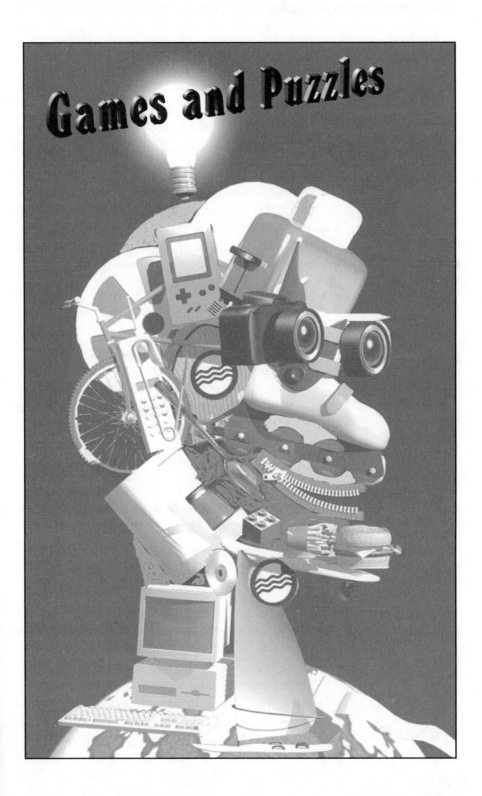

Games and Puzzles

GAMES AND PUZZLES

Name These Games or Puzzles . . .

1. What a challenge! It has 43 quintillion solutions and it might take you days to line up the colours, but it took the inventor only two minutes to do the job.

2. Originally this game was called Criss-Cross. To win, it helps if you know your Qs and Ps — they're worth more than Es and Os.

3. The inventors took only 45 minutes to design the game board, but years to collect its 6000 questions. It was worth the effort! This game has been such a hot seller that today the inventors are millionaires.

4. Too complicated . . . too long . . . too boring . . . Those were just a few of the fifty-two reasons Parker Brothers originally gave for refusing to carry this game. Good thing Parker Brothers changed its mind. For over sixty years, this game has been its biggest seller.

5. Named after a Hawaiian fruit drink, this collecting, stacking, and slamming game is likely based on an ancient Japanese one.

ANSWERS on page 96.

Before there was television, some parents placed a bowl of goldfish in a child's sick room, to keep the invalid amused.

Bingo

Tired and depressed. That's how toy salesman Edwin Lowe felt as he drove to Jacksonville, Florida, one night in 1929. Along the way he spotted the bright lights of a carnival and stopped to investigate. He wandered into a tent filled with people seated at tables and surrounded by numbered cards and stacks of beans. At another table an announcer called numbers, and as he did, players put beans on corresponding squares on the cards. When five squares in a row were covered, the player called "Beano" and received a Kewpie doll as a prize.

Lowe was so taken by the game that he tried it out when he got home. One young winner became so excited that instead of calling out "Beano" he stammered "B-b-b-bingo!" The name stuck. Lowe produced a commercial version of the game and made it popular around the country, and today thousands of communities use Bingo as a source of fun — and funds.

Crossword Puzzle

Editor Arthur Wynne had a problem. He had a deadline to meet. The Sunday edition of his newspaper was about to go to print, and he still had space to fill.

Wynne picked up a pencil and idly scribbled words on a piece of paper. He wrote one word, then used one of its letters to link to another word. Before long he had a pattern of words, some written horizontally, others vertically, but each linked to a common letter of another word.

The arrangement gave Wynne an idea. He erased some of the words, leaving empty spaces. Then he wrote clues for the missing words. That way readers would have to guess the words from the clues and the number of empty spaces left behind. The words crossed each other so Wynne called his puzzle the "wordcross game."

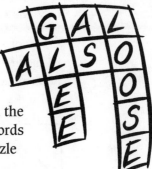

The first of Wynne's puzzles appeared in the *New York World* newspaper on December 21, 1913. Readers loved it from the start, and before long "crossword puzzles" became a feature in newspapers around the world.

SPOTLIGHT ON INVENTION

Shrink or Enlarge an
Existing Invention to Make a New One

I invent nothing. I rediscover.

— Auguste Rodin

THE INVENTION OF MINIATURE GOLF

How a Mini-Version Became a Maxi-Hit

John Carter of Chattanooga, Tennessee, golfed whenever possible. He loved the game! Unfortunately, a game of golf took hours to complete and was expensive to play. Carter had neither the money nor the time to play as often as he liked. Figuring there had to be a way to make the game more practical and less costly, he did some hard thinking.

As it was for many people, putting was Carter's favourite part of golf. Why not keep putting in the game, he thought, and take the rest out? With that in mind he invented a new game of golf. He shrank the size of the course, set up a series of obstacles, and gave the players only one club — a putter.

Carter opened his first course in the 1920s. He named his invention Tom Thumb Golf, after a famous circus midget. Most people called it miniature golf, the name we use today.

 Other Shrunken or Enlarged Inventions

Ferris Wheel As a boy, George Washington Ferris, an American engineer, admired the big paddle boats that chugged down the Carson River in Nevada. When planners for the 1892 World's Exposition

---

announced that they were looking for a central attraction at least as spectacular as the Eiffel Tower in Paris, Ferris thought back to his childhood days. He adapted the paddle wheel design, producing a giant turning upright wheel. The first Ferris wheel cost $385,000 to build. It rose about seventy-five metres above the ground, had 36 glass-enclosed cars attached to its rim, and was driven by two 1000-horse-power steam engines. At full capacity, 2000 passengers could ride the wheel at one time. Although the original wheel was dismantled in 1904, the idea caught on and soon Ferris wheels were the main attractions at fairs and expositions around the world.

See Also . . .
Erector Sets (page 107)
Lincoln Logs (page 106)
IMAX (page 52)

Monopoly

Charles Darrow's dream was to become rich. Fabulously rich. So rich that he would never have to work another day in his life. But in 1933 the down-and-out engineer was a long way from his goal. Darrow didn't have a steady job, and with a wife and children to support, times were tough. For awhile he did anything he could to make ends meet, but he knew he could never become rich this way.

The surest way to instant wealth, Darrow figured, was to invent something. So he quit looking for work and spent all of his time tinkering in his home. He invented a combination bat and ball. Then he devised a simplified scoring

pad for bridge players. No one was interested in either invention. Then one night a friend of Darrow's wife brought a homemade game called Monopoly into the Darrow home. The game had been invented twenty years earlier by a woman named Elizabeth (Lizzie) Magie. The aim of the game was to buy property as players moved around a game board.

The game fascinated Darrow, and he decided to make his own out of some leftover linoleum. He changed the original design a little and colour-coded different properties on the board. For the game pieces he carved bits of scrap wood.

When friends saw Darrow's game, they begged him to make one for them too. He did. After all, he didn't have anything better to do with his time. Word got around and soon he could hardly keep up with the demand. But it took an entire day to make a single set, and Darrow sold each one for just four dollars, so he realized he had to change his way of operating.

Darrow had two choices. Start his own company to make the game, or look for an existing company to sell it. Starting a company was risky and required money. Instead, Darrow decided to approach Parker Brothers, one of the largest game manufacturers in the United States. Parker Brothers turned Darrow down flat. They figured Monopoly would never sell. The game was too complicated and took too long to play, and the board was poorly designed, they said. In all, they listed fifty-two weaknesses of the game.

But Darrow was not discouraged. He borrowed money and hired printers to manufacture 5000 Monopoly sets. They sold quickly, so he ordered more. When the executives at Parker Brothers heard of Darrow's success, they had second thoughts. In 1935 they bought the rights from Darrow, as well as the rights to Lizzie Magie's earlier version of the game.

Darrow became a millionaire. With his fortune he

retired to a farm, travelled the globe collecting exotic flowers, and never invented another game in his life.

As for Parker Brothers, it hit the jackpot too. In the first year of production the company was flooded with so many orders that they had to be stacked in laundry baskets and stored in hallways. Since that time Monopoly has outsold every other game handled by the company.

POG

Collect 'em. Stack 'em. Slam 'em.

POGs became wildly popular in the early 1990s, but the game may be much older than it seems. Six hundred years old, in fact.

Centuries ago the Japanese played a game called menkos. In this game, kids stacked and flipped small etched disks of clay, wood, or ceramic. Japanese immigrants to Maui, one of the Hawaiian islands, brought menkos with them around the turn of the century. But on Maui, they found a cheaper, more convenient source of stackable disks.

At the time, milk was delivered in bottles, each one sealed with a waxed cardboard disk. Springy, sturdy milkcaps seemed perfect for slamming and stacking. And since different dairies printed different designs and logos on them, milkcaps made great items for collecting and trading, too.

Chinese checkers was invented in England, not China.

In the early 1990s, the Haleakala Dairy on the Hawaiian island of Maui produced a new fruit drink called Passion Orange Guava. To promote the juice the company printed "POG" in bright red letters on the caps of its old-fashioned bottles. Kids on Maui collected the caps and called their game POG.

POG might have remained a local game if it hadn't been for Blossom Glabisco, a Honolulu teacher who grew up on Maui. To keep the interest of her bored

and restless students, Glabisco taught them the stacking, slamming game she remembered from her childhood. Her niece brought POG milkcaps from Maui, and soon kids all over Hawaii were playing and collecting POGs. Printers caught wind of the game and designed new milkcaps to keep up with the demand. By 1993 an estimated 1 billion POGs had found their way around the islands of Hawaii. Visitors to Hawaii bought POGs, too. In a few short years, the POG craze spread worldwide.

SPOTLIGHT ON INVENTION

Add a New Feature or Part to an Existing Invention

Invention breeds invention.

— Ralph Waldo Emerson

THE PUZZ-3D STORY

How an Old Idea Spawned a New One

Jigsaw puzzles have been around a long time. John Spilsbury, a British teacher, invented them in the 1760s as a way of teaching his students mapping skills.

Paul Gallant, a Montreal inventor, gave the jigsaw puzzle a new twist. He worked for a marketing firm that sold toys and games. He was producing a new jigsaw puzzle when an idea popped into his mind. Why not make a 3-D jigsaw puzzle, one that had shape and could stand upright on its own? That way the finished puzzle could be displayed on a shelf. He tried using cardboard, but it didn't work. Then in 1990 a few sheets of polyethylene foam were delivered to his office. The foam was supposed to be used for another product, but as soon as he saw it, Gallant thought of the 3-D puzzle. Using a computer-enhanced image he glued a design on the foam, then cut the sheet into interlocking pieces and assembled them. The foam worked. When he was finished, Gallant had a sturdy, towering form on the table in front of him.

For other "addition" inventions see:
Pencil (page 139)
Safety Pin (page 143)

Rubik's Cube

In the early 1970s Enro Rubik, a professor at the Academy of Applied Arts in Budapest, Hungary, noticed the difficulty his students had understanding complicated ideas in mathematics. He figured that if his students could handle and twist a solid shape into new combinations of colour and design, they would learn mathematics more easily.

In his spare time, Rubik designed a six-coloured cube. At first glance it looked simple: six moveable faces, each able to rotate on its centre with a simple twist, each face split into nine small cubes. But it was the combination of colour and movement that made Rubik's invention a challenge. Each corner cube could be turned in three possible directions, and because each cube had three colours on its sides, a single twist produced a different arrangement of colours.

It took only a few twists to scramble the colours. Once scrambled, however, could the original pattern be restored? That was the challenge of Rubik's Cube. When people got their hands on the cube they couldn't put it down. They were hooked, and that's what gave Rubik the idea that his invention might be more than just a tool for mathematics.

In 1977 a Hungarian company began selling Rubik's Cube. Then in 1980 the Ideal Toy Corporation bought the rights. Soon the cube craze spread around the globe.

CUBE FACTS

The label on Rubik's Cube says, "There are three billion positions, but only one solution." In actual fact, there are 43,252,003,274, 489,856,000 positions. That's about 43 quintillion!

To solve Rubik's Cube, the user must think like a computer programmer: first breaking the solution into small sequences, then breaking those into even smaller sequences.

Many people take days to solve the puzzle. Rubik himself was able to do it in about two minutes.

Scrabble

Alfred Botts loved games. He also loved crossword puzzles, so in 1931 the unemployed architect combined the two into one. He invented a word game that used 100 wooden tiles, each painted with a letter of the alphabet. Players pulled letters at random and tried to link words to those of their opponents.

Botts called his game Criss-Cross. For more than a decade, he played it at home with family and friends. Over time he improved his game, perfecting the rules and adding point values to the letters so players could keep score.

In 1948, with encouragement from a friend, James Brunot, Botts copyrighted his game and changed its name to Scrabble. The two men started producing the game in an abandoned schoolhouse. At first business was slow; then in the summer of 1952 sales boomed. In only two years sales soared from less than 10,000 games a year to more than 4 million. Botts and Brunot couldn't manufacture games fast enough to keep up with the demand. Finally they sold the rights to Selchow-Righter, a game manufacturing company.

Today, over a half century after its invention, Scrabble remains as popular as ever.

SCRABBLE FACTS

Over 2 million Scrabble sets are sold each year.

Scrabble tiles are made from Vermont maple.

What's a *qoph*? It's one of five "Q" words that do not need a "U." The others are *faqir, qaid, qindar,* and *qintar.*

Scrabble has 3.2 billion possible seven-letter combinations.

FIVE OTHER GAMES

Five Games That Date Back More Than 1000 Years
Bowling Although games requiring players to hit standing objects have been around for thousands of years, German monks gave the game a new twist around A.D. 300. Wanting some way to prove their devotion to God, they set up a bottle-shaped object called a

kegel, or devil. Then, from a distance, they rolled a ball and tried knocking the kegel down. By striking it, the monks renounced sin and declared their belief in God.

Eventually the religious practice became a popular game. More kegels or pins were added, and by the 1600s a version known as nine-pin was being played around Europe. In time, another pin was added to create ten-pin — the modern bowling game.

In 1904 Tommy Ryan, a Canadian inventor and owner of a bowling alley, gave the game another twist. Since many bowlers tried to fit in a game during their lunch break, Ryan reduced the number of pins to five and shrank the ball to a fraction of its size. People liked the shorter, less strenuous game, and soon its popularity spread across Canada.

Checkers A form of checkers was played in ancient Egypt almost 4000 years ago. Bits of the game have been found in Egyptian tombs. The two-player game involved enemy pieces, captures, and war-like moves. Later civilizations adapted the game, adding "kings" and "crowns" to make checkers what it is today.

Chess Ancient Persians played a chess-like game in the fifth century A.D., but chess pieces dating as far back as A.D. 200 have been found elsewhere in Asia. The game was brought to Europe at the time of the Crusades.

Marbles Today marbles are mass-produced from glass, but the earliest ones were smoothed stones or the rounded knucklebones of dogs and sheep. Archeologists have found sets of marbles in Egyptian tombs, proving that some form of the game existed as far back as 3000 B.C.

Snakes and Ladders Also called Chutes and Ladders, this game originated in India centuries ago, with Hindus who used it to teach their children about the evil and goodness encountered on life's journey. The game came to North America with early English settlers and was first mass produced in 1943.

Trivial Pursuit

Trivial Pursuit was born in a Montreal kitchen on December 15, 1979. Scott Abbott, a sportswriter, and Chris Haney, a photo editor for another newspaper, were sitting around the kitchen table talking about games when a friendly argument started: Who was the better Scrabble player? There was only one way to settle the argument. Play a game.

Haney went out to purchase a Scrabble game, then realized that it was the sixth one he had bought in his life. Then and there the two men decided to invent a game of their own that was would be just as challenging and just as much fun. Within forty-five minutes, they had a basic plan for a new game. It combined the action of a board game with the excitement of a quiz show.

Neither man had experience in manufacturing and sales, so they visited the Canadian Toy and Decoration Fair in Montreal, posing as a reporter and photographer. They browsed through displays and asked questions of toy manufacturers. With their new-found information they set up their own company, and contacted suppliers to manufacture different parts of the game.

The hardest part still lay ahead, however: gathering the trivia questions. The men spent five months poring through encyclopedias, guides, and almanacs to assemble the thousands of questions, selecting ones that weren't too obvious, but not too difficult either.

With money raised from friends, relatives, and former workers, Abbot and Haney produced 1200 sets of Trivial Pursuit. In November, 1981, the games were shipped to stores around Vancouver and Toronto. In a few weeks all the games were sold.

Abbott and Haney ordered another 20,000 games; then, when these sold, another 80,000. The game was a runaway success. By the Christmas season of 1982, people lined up for blocks in front of stores to purchase the game. Since that time, millions of sets have been sold worldwide.

Video Games

Anyone who has ever played Super Mario Brothers, Mortal Kombat, Donkey Kong, or other video games should know about Willy Higinbotham. As near as anyone can tell, he invented the first video game.

In the 1950s Higinbotham worked as a physicist for Brookhaven National Laboratory in Upton, New York. Brookhaven was a government nuclear research laboratory involved in top-secret developments. Once each year, though, it held an open house and invited visitors to browse through the facility. Usually its displays featured photographs, descriptions and bits and pieces of equipment. Pretty boring, Higinbotham figured. There had to be some way to liven it up.

A few weeks before the 1958 open house he rummaged through some spare equipment and found an oscilloscope (a type of early TV picture tube) plus a small analog computer, wires, switches, and other electronic gear. He figured out how to hook the computer to the oscilloscope to make a bouncing ball appear on the screen: a two-player tennis game, of sorts. He gave each player a box with a button and a knob. A push of the button fired the ball into the

Ralph Baer, an engineer, was one of the first people to see the commercial possibilities of video games. While waiting for a New York City bus on September 1, 1966, Baer thought about a money-making idea. Since there were millions and millions of television sets around the country, why not make games to be played on them? In his spare time he produced a basic game involving one spot chasing another around the screen.

Three months later he showed his game to company officials, and with the help of other engineers developed a video hockey game and a paddle and ball game. Baer and his colleagues spent several years perfecting the games and finally received a patent in 1972, about the same time Atari released Pong.

opponent's court. A twist of the knob controlled the height of the ball.

The electronic tennis game was set up in the company gym in a far-off corner under a basketball hoop. Hardly noticeable, it seemed, but before long people flocked to his display to try the game out.

For the 1959 open house Higinbotham improved the game. He rigged it so that the gravitational pull on the ball could be changed. Visitors could play tennis on the moon (low gravity) or on Jupiter (high gravity). Once again the game was a hit. Eventually Higinbotham tired of tinkering with the game, though. He never patented it.

In 1971, Atari Inc. marketed Pong, the first ever commercial video game. In it, two players whack a ball over a net, a game very similar to Willy Higinbotham's. Pong, a runaway success, spawned dozens of other video games, and started the electronic game craze.

TWO MORE GAMES

Candyland When Eleanor Abbott was stricken with polio and confined to bed, she put her time to good use. She devised a game based on matching colours and shapes. Since its introduction in 1949, more than 20 million sets of Candyland have been sold.

Twister Twister, the Milton Bradley game that forces the human body into pretzel-like shapes, became wildly popular after it was demonstrated on the Tonight Show in 1966. Viewers watched host Johnny Carson and entertainer Eva Gabor play, then rushed out the next day to buy their own. That year alone over 3 million Twister games were sold.

ANSWERS TO NAME THESE GAMES AND PUZZLES:
1. Rubik's Cube 2. Scrabble 3. Trivial Pursuit 4. Monopoly
5. POG

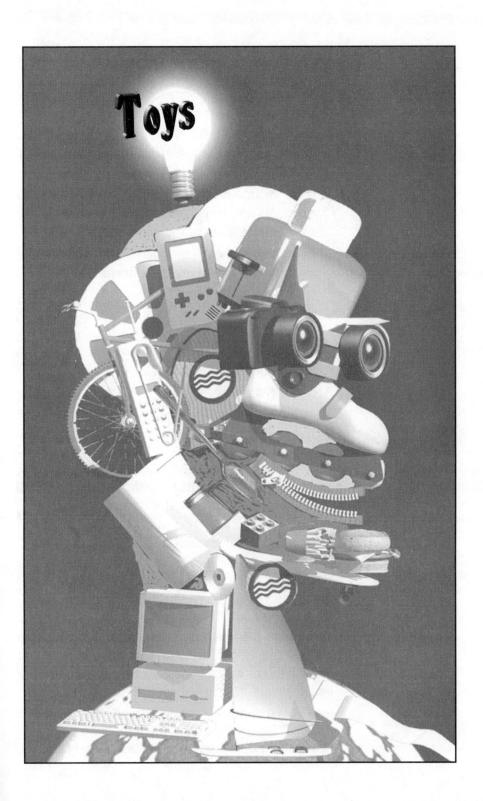

TOYS

Name These Toys:

1. First it was a pie tin. Next it was a flying saucer. Now it's a popular toy, sport and game all rolled into one.

2. It's a toy and more! This sticky, stretchy stuff also removes lint, levels lopsided chairs, and lifts cartoons right out of the newspaper.

3. Its Danish name means "play well." Millions of users agree. The many parts of this toy can be combined in countless ways.

4. Hundreds of years ago, this toy was a deadly weapon used by hunters in the Philippines. Nowadays its up-and-down motion provides fun for kids around the world.

ANSWERS on page 113.

Ant Farm

At a family picnic in 1956, Milton Levine noticed a group of children huddled together near a backyard pool. Curious, he investigated. "I saw a bunch of ants around the pool," he said. "I saw a bunch of kids, and they were interested in the ants. And it came to me."

Levine mounted two sheets of clear plastic in a frame, and filled the gap between them with sand. He added a fistful of ants and watched, fascinated, as the ants tunnelled through the sand. Levine called his creation an ant farm. To make it more farm-like, he added tiny plastic figures: a barn, farmhouse, silo, and windmill. He read about ants and prepared an instruction manual to go along with the ant farm.

To sell his invention, Levine took out a small newspaper ad. "Watch the ants dig tunnels and build

---

ANT FARM FACTS

To keep up with the demand, Uncle Milton Industries hires ant catchers. Some catchers use straws to blow ants out of their tunnels. Some use shovels to dig them out. One even uses a car vacuum to suck up ants.

bridges," it read. The response was overwhelming. Orders for ant farms poured in, and Milton Levine was in business.

Since then over 12 million ant farms have been sold, and each year Uncle Milton Industries, Levine's company, ships 15 million ants to curious boys and girls.

Barbie Doll

By any account, Ruth Handler and her husband, Elliot, had it all in the 1950s: two terrific children, a spacious home in Los Angeles, a thriving toymaking business. But it was Ruth's invention that gave the Handlers even more success and made their toy company, Mattel, famous around the world.

She got the idea for her invention by watching her daughter at play. Like most girls her age, Barbara had dolls. Cute, cuddly baby-sized dolls. But she hardly played with them. Instead she spent hours in her room dressing and outfitting her adult-looking paper dolls. Armed with a variety of cut-out paper clothes, she could change her dolls' appearance at a moment's notice.

Too bad she couldn't do that with a real doll, Handler thought. A grown-up looking doll. One that came with its own dresses and accessories. With that idea in mind she designed a doll and a series of clothes and accessories to match. She called the doll Barbie, after her daughter.

Barbie made her first public appearance at the New York Toy Show in 1959. The reaction was disappointing. "It won't sell," Handler was told again and again.

But Barbie did sell, better than anyone expected. So successful was the doll that in 1961 Mattel introduced a male doll to accompany her. He was called Ken, after the Handlers' son.

BARBIE FACTS

Since Barbie dolls first hit the market in 1959, over 400 million have been sold worldwide.

Barbie has a last name. Officially, she is Barbie Roberts.

To be sure Barbie wears the newest fashions, Mattel sends its people to Europe each year to view the latest collections of world-famous designers. Mattel's designers then produce scaled-down Barbie-sized outfits.

The first Barbie dolls cost only three dollars. Today these dolls can be worth over $1000 as collector's items, if they are in mint condition.

What was the key to Ruth Handler's success? She explained it this way: "I guess I learned to observe people in their daily lives, and every once in a while, I identify a need."

G.I. Joe: The Undoll Barbie was a great toy for girls. But would boys play with a similar toy? People decided that if it was known as a doll, they wouldn't. But call it a soldier . . . In 1963 Don Levine, a designer for Hasbro Toys, got the idea that a toy soldier would be ideal for boys. But there were lots of toy soldiers being sold already. Most of these were small, plastic action figures that could be set up in various battle situations. Levine wanted his soldier to be different.

One day while browsing through an art store he happened to see a display of wooden artist's figures. The figures had hinged joints so they could be propped up in any number of poses, giving the artist a chance to sketch the human figure in any position. Levine bought a dozen of the figures and dressed them in a variety of soldier costumes. To make the face, he and the designers at Hasbro studied photographs of twenty Medal of Honor recipients. Taking the strongest features of each one, they created a rugged-looking soldier, complete with battle scar on the right cheek.

The figure needed a name, however. One night Levine saw *The Story of G.I. Joe*, a 1945 movie. G.I. meant "general infantry," a popular term for foot soldier. Levine thought the name was perfect, and in 1964 Hasbro began selling G.I. Joe.

Hasbro followed some of the same marketing strategies as Mattel did with Barbie. G.I. Joe

G

had twenty-one moving parts, was roughly the
same size as Barbie, and came with a world of
accessories, everything from dog tags and
weapons to a jeep. Boys, many of whom
would not play with a doll, adopted G.I. Joe
as one of their favourite toys. In the first year,
sales of G.I. Joe topped $16.9 million.

Frisbee

Tossing a disk is not exactly a new idea. Ancient
Greeks included a disk-throwing event in the earliest
Olympic Games held over 2700 years ago. But
tossing a disk, catching it, and tossing it back? Now,
that's a much more recent pastime.

In the 1870s a New England man, William Russell
Frisbie, operated a thriving bakery, the Frisbie Pie
Company. Frisbie's pies were well known, not only
for their great taste, but also for the round metal pie
plates that held them.

The tin containers were supposed to be returned to
the Frisbie Pie Company after the pie was eaten, but
students at the nearby university had other plans.
Someone had discovered that with a quick flick of
the wrist the empty pie plate could be made to sail,
swoop and hover through the air. Rather than
returning the containers to be recycled, students used
them for a simple game of toss and catch. The plates
were heavy, though, and could cause injuries if they
struck someone. To alert passersby to the danger, it
became the custom to yell "Frisbie!" as the plate was
tossed.

For decades the pie plate game remained a college
fad largely unknown to the rest of the world. Then in
the early 1950s an enterprising Californian inventor,
Walter Frederick Morrison, brought it into the open.
Morrison didn't know about the pie plate game, but

he did know that people were fascinated with outer space. UFOs, Martians, flying saucers — those were the most popular topics at the time. Aiming to cash in on this interest, Morrison invented a plastic flying saucer toy. Then he rented a booth at a local county fair to sell it.

He used an amazing sales pitch. Above the heads of onlookers he and an assistant unravelled an invisible wire. "Make way for the wire!" he'd shout to get everyone's attention. Then, with the assistant holding one end of the imaginary wire and Morrison holding the other, he'd release the plastic disk. The crowd watched in awe as the flying saucer floated over their heads, suspended it seemed by the invisible wire.

After the demonstration people were eager to buy their own flying saucers. Morrison gladly gave them away free, but with one money-making catch. To make the saucer work, he told people, they needed the wire, too, and that he sold in bundles of about thirty metres for a dollar.

Morrison continued to improve his design, changing its shape and weight to improve its flight. He called it the Pluto Platter and advertised it as the "flip-fly away" toy. In 1955 officials of the Wham-O Toy Company noticed his disk, invited him to join forces, and in 1957 began producing and selling the Pluto Platter.

At first, sales were slow. Enter the metal pie plate. On a trip to the East Coast, one of the Wham-O owners heard of the game of toss and catch — "Frisbee" — that students had been playing for decades. He liked the name so much he changed the name of the Pluto Platter to Frisbee (not realizing that the original spelling was Frisbie). As the popularity of the toy grew in the 1960s, Wham-O sponsored a series of Frisbee tournaments that made the toy into a popular sport too.

The earliest false teeth had springs to keep the teeth in place.

Five Toys That Originated 3000 Years Ago or More

Top The earliest tops were likely invented in Babylon over 5000 years ago. The Japanese later improved the design by adding holes around the outside of the top to make it hum and whistle as it spun.

Yo-yo A Chinese invention, the first yo-yo dates back to 1000 B.C. It was made of two ivory disks connected by a peg and a silk cord. In the sixteenth century hunters in the Philippines adapted the toy as a weapon. The killer yo-yo was made from heavy wooden disks, or sometimes chipped rock, and sturdy twine. The hunter stood in a tree, twirled the weapon and tossed it. If the thrower's aim was accurate, the weapon wound itself around the legs of the animal being hunted. If the aim was off, the hunter could pull the weapon back easily.

Over time the weapon came to be used as a toy only. In the late 1920s Donald Duncan, an American businessman visiting the Philippines, saw it in use. He started manufacturing yo-yos, and since 1929 his company has sold more than a half billion!

Kite These colourful flyers were first used in China around 1200 B.C. as way of sending coded messages between troops during battles. Over the centuries the Chinese perfected kite design, making them larger and more colourful, and adding tails to improve balance. Kites later spread to India, then, by the twelfth century, to Europe.

Rattle Toy rattles have been found in Egyptian children's tombs dating back to 1360 B.C. Made of clay and stuffed with pebbles, many were shaped like birds, bears and other animals. Their most common colour was sky blue, a colour that held magical powers for the Egyptians.

Hula Hoop As far back as 1000 B.C., Egyptian, Greek and Roman children made hoops from dried grapevines. The hoops were sometimes rolled along the ground, pushed by sticks. Other times they were tossed into the air, caught, and twirled around the waist.

Australians used a bamboo version of the hoop as an exercise ring in gym classes. In 1957 officials of Wham-O, the company that later produced the Frisbee, saw the Australian hoop in use. They adapted the idea, and added a plastic ring to their line of toys, calling it the Hula Hoop because people's hip-rotating motion resembled the Hawaiian hula dance.

The Hula Hoop was an overnight success. People loved the toy and bought it faster than it could be made. In 1958 alone Wham-O sold over 20 million. The fad was short-lived, though. By the next year, sales began to drop, and the Hula Hoop craze was over.

Lego

With Lego, anything is possible, some say. Small wonder! Two eight-studded plastic bricks of the same colour can be joined in twenty-four different ways; six bricks can be combined in 102,981,500 ways! Now add other pieces, bricks of different size and colour, gears, wheels, hinges, tiny human figures, and the combinations are endless!

Lego was the brainchild of Ole Kirk Christiansen, a Danish carpenter born in 1891. When he was six, tending sheep in the fields around his village, he carved whistles and small figures out of wood to pass the time. Later he learned woodworking skills from an older brother and opened his own carpentry shop in the village of Billund. He built houses, furniture, doors, and windows. To see how full-sized objects worked, Christiansen often made smaller scale models. He loved this side of his business, and began selling doll houses, building bricks, and other wooden toys.

Soon Christiansen manufactured only toys, so it was time to choose a new name for the company. He combined two Danish words, *leg godt* ("play well") and came up with the name Lego.

Christiansen had high standards. He wanted his toys to be sturdy and long lasting. Over and over he told his children, who helped in the shop, "Det bedste er ikke for godt," which means "Only the best is good enough." Once his son, Godtfred, thought he would save time and money by skipping a coat of paint on some toys. When Christiansen found out, he had Godtfred unpackage the toys and spend the night painting them again.

The company produced its first plastic bricks in 1949, but it wasn't until 1958 that Lego came out with its present stud-and-tube design. With this unique system, the tiny cylinders on one side of a building brick lock around the hollow tubes at the bottom of another. This enables the bricks to stay together, yet permits them to be taken apart with a simple tug and twist.

The new design proved so popular the company was flooded with orders. In 1969 a second line of bricks was introduced. Duplo bricks were larger, eight times the size of regular Lego. That made them easier and safer for younger children to use. Later, Lego Technic, a more advanced and complex line,

LEGO FACTS

Lego is made in twelve colours, but the main ones are white, yellow, red, blue, and black.

To make Lego, acrylonitrile butadiene styrene granules are melted into a paste under strict conditions of heat and pressure. The paste is then injected into moulds to harden.

A theme park made from over 33 million pieces of Lego has become one of Denmark's largest tourist attractions. Legoland Park, in Christiansen's hometown of Billund, covers ten hectares and has hundreds of exhibits, all made from Lego. Visitors can see replicas of famous buildings and cities, roam through Lego-made gardens and streets, ride a "merry-Lego-round," or stop at a play centre to build their own Lego creations.

was added for older children.

Although Christiansen died in 1958, Lego still remains a family company. First Godtfred took charge, then in 1979 his son, Kjeld Kirk Christiansen, took over. Today, Kjeld's own three children help out, learning like their father and grandfather the lesson taught by Ole Kirk Christiansen: Only the best is good enough.

Three Other Construction Toy Favourites

Tinkertoy

The idea for Tinkertoy came to its inventor, Charles Pajeau, in 1913, after he watched children playing with pencils, sticks, and empty spools of thread. Working in a garage behind his house, he designed a wooden construction set that had coloured sticks, connecting pieces, wheels, and moving parts.

Pajeau packed the set in a cylinder and called it Tinkertoy. In 1914 he tried selling his invention at the American Toy Fair. No one was interested. Then at Christmastime he had a bright idea. Using midgets dressed as elves, Pajeau had them play with Tinkertoys in the display windows of New York's Grand Central Station. The promotion caused a huge traffic jam, but the stunt worked. A year later over a million sets had been sold, and since 1914 over 100 million Tinkertoy kits have been sold worldwide.

Lincoln Logs

When American architect Frank Lloyd Wright went to Tokyo in 1916 to supervise the building of a new earthquake-proof hotel, he brought his twenty-year-old son John along. The hotel was being constructed using ancient Japanese wood-fitting methods, and while John watched huge timbers being joined together he got an idea. When he got back home he designed a new construction set with interlocking wooden logs that could be used to build forts, cabins and houses. He called the toy Lincoln Logs. It has been a big hit with children ever since. A half million sets of Lincoln Logs are sold each year.

Erector Set

A. C. Gilbert got the idea for this toy after watching some workmen constructing a high-tension tower in 1912. Fascinated by the steel girders that made up the tower's frame, Gilbert experimented with a scaled-down version at home. He cut strips of cardboard, punched holes in them and tried fastening them together with nuts and bolts. Satisfied with his basic idea, he had some cast in steel at a machine shop, then assembled a kit of various parts and pieces, added wheels, angles and plates, and sold it under the name Erector Set. The line now includes some recent versions: Mega Claw Excavator, Alien Terrain Patrol and other space-age kits.

The 1950's saw the rise (and fall) of more new toy inventions: Mr. Potato Head, Betsy Wetsy, and Davy Crockett hats.

GOOGOLPLEX

Googolplex When Canadian architect Harry Erickson grew tired of cutting and constructing cardboard models to demonstrate his design ideas, he didn't quit. Instead he invented a new small-scale building device he called Googolplex.

The key to Googolplex is its unique double hinge and its many geometric shapes. By linking pieces and giving them a twist or a turn, a builder can make plastic models of almost any shape and size.

Domes, castles, robots, space stations, flat

shapes or three dimensional — with Googolplex the possibilities are limited only by the imagination.

That's one of the reasons Erickson chose Googolplex for a name. To mathematicians, a googol is the number one followed by 100 zeros. A googolplex is one followed by a googol of zeros. In other words, one followed by a billion zeros. A very large number!

Although Erickson invented Googolplex to help with architectural designs, it didn't take long for his idea to inspire others. Since the 1980s when it was first introduced, Googolplex has proved popular with young and old alike. It has also been used in schools to teach geometry and problem solving, in film studios to construct mockups of props, and by various manufacturers to train employees in production techniques.

SILLY PUTTY FACTS

Since its invention, some practical uses for Silly Putty have been found:

It can remove lint and hair from clothes and furniture.

Athletes can knead it between their fingers to build up muscles in their hands and forearms.

A wad of Silly Putty under the leg of a wobbly chair or table straightens it.

If pressed onto comics in a newspaper, Silly Putty will "lift" the image onto itself.

The astronauts of *Apollo 8* used it to keep their tools from floating around inside the spacecraft.

SPOTLIGHT ON INVENTION

Find a Use for Something That Seems Useless

There is one thing stronger than all the armies in the world, and that is an idea whose time has come.

—Victor Hugo

THE INVENTION OF SILLY PUTTY

How Useless Goo Found Its Purpose

No moving parts! No fancy electronics! Just a simple ball of goo! Even so, Silly Putty remains one of the most popular toys ever invented by accident. In 1945 James Wright, an engineer working for General Electric, was asked to find a way to make synthetic rubber. Wright tried mixing different chemicals. One day he combined boric acid with silicone oil and produced a sticky substance with unusual properties.

The new compound was gooey and elastic. It could be stretched farther and bounced higher than rubber. When whacked by a hammer, the stuff shattered. Yet it could be moulded into odd shapes, and it kept its bounce under a wide range of temperatures. The substance was not a good substitute for rubber, though. It was too stretchy and sticky. In fact, none of the scientists at General Electric could find any practical way of using it. Finally the company mailed samples of the strange material to engineers around the world in the hopes that someone would figure out what to do with it.

By chance, a wad of it ended up at a party attended by Paul Hodgson, an advertising man. Hodgson had been putting together a catalogue for a toy store. When he saw adults at the party acting like children, tossing and stretching the stuff around the room, he decided to include the "nutty putty" in the catalogue. The results were surprising. Nutty Putty outsold every other item in the catalogue except crayons. Hodgson realized he had a winner. He borrowed $147 and bought a chunk of the stuff from General Electric. He  changed the name to Silly Putty, and hired a student to separate it into one-ounce balls (about thirty grams) and package them in plastic egg-like containers.

Silly Putty was an overnight success. In the first five years alone, over 32 million containers of it were sold worldwide.

Another Useless-Turned-Useful Invention

Blue Jeans Levi Strauss, a young peddler, headed to California during the 1849 Gold Rush loaded with goods to sell. He brought along huge supplies of canvas which he expected miners would want for tents and wagon covers. He was wrong. No one wanted the canvas, and he was left with bolts of the material. But Strauss was an observant man. Prospectors, he noticed, needed sturdy pants. He hired a tailor to sew pants from the leftover canvas. They sold quickly, and soon he was in the fashion business. Eventually he switched from canvas to denim, and dyed the material blue so that one piece of cloth would match the next. At first, people called the pants "blue denims," then later "blue jeans" — slang for Genoa, a town in Italy where a denim-like material was made.

Slinky

It flips. It flops. It slithers and crawls. It's Slinky, the springy toy invented almost by accident.

A shipyard engineer, Richard James, was given a problem to solve. It seemed that as waves rocked ships at sea, the needles on the ship's instruments jiggled, making them difficult to read accurately. Find some way of reducing the vibrations on the ship's instruments, James was told.

He figured that if he attached springs to the instruments there would be fewer vibrations. He was hard at work experimenting with different kinds of springs when something odd happened. One spring fell off a high shelf. Instead of crashing to the floor, as expected, it slowly uncoiled, flopped onto a pile of books, snaked down to a desk, then hopped to the floor. Amazed, James took the spring home to show his wife, Betty. "I think I can make a toy out of this," he told her.

The Jameses wanted just the right name for their toy. Something catchy, easy to remember. Betty searched through the dictionary, looking for a word to describe the spring's slithering action. Slinky seemed perfect.

In the beginning, Slinky didn't sell. Then one evening in 1945 Betty and Richard demonstrated their toy in a department store. A mob of people surrounded them, waving dollar bills in the air. In just ninety minutes, they sold 400 Slinkys. Since then millions of Slinkys have slithered and hopped their way into homes around the world.

More Toy Bits

Matchbox Toys

In 1952 the owners of a British die-casting factory decided to expand their business by manufacturing toys on the side. Their first product was a miniature reproduction of Princess Elizabeth's Royal Coach. Sales were modest at first, but the following year, when Elizabeth became Queen, business boomed. With that success, the owners went into the toy business full-time, manufacturing a line of tiny models called Matchbox Toys. Why the name? Because each figure was just small enough to fit into a matchbox.

Model Trains

Trains always fascinated Joshua Lionel Cowen. At the age of seven he carved a wooden model of a locomotive and tried fitting it with a tiny steam engine. Unfortunately, the train exploded, spewing splinters of wood in all directions.

As an adult, Cowen kept up his interest in trains.

He invented a small battery-powered motor that he fitted into a small flatcar he had designed. Then he constructed a nine-metre circular brass track for the car to ride on. Cowen packaged the whole set and convinced a small shop to display it. The train proved popular and in time Cowen added cattle cars, coal cars, passenger cars, and other parts. In 1903 he issued his first catalogue. The Lionel Train Company has been in business ever since.

Play-Doh

Sometimes it pays to listen to others. It worked for Joseph McVicker. In 1955 he got the idea for a new product by paying attention to a nursery school teacher's complaints. The teacher had complained that modelling clay was too stiff to be rolled by young students. Besides, it dried out quickly and was unusable in a short time. McVicker mixed up a new modelling compound, one that was softer, more flexible, and didn't harden quickly. He called it Play-Doh.

McVicker's father owned Rainbow Crafts, a Cincinnati, Ohio, company that specialized in soaps and cleaners. McVicker convinced his father to add Play-Doh to its product line. To advertise it the McVickers set up a booth at an educator's convention. The wife of a department store owner saw Play-Doh and convinced her husband to sell it in his store. Play-Doh was an instant success, and in no time, it was being sold in stores everywhere.

Some products are named for the sounds they make. Two examples: Ping Pong and zipper.

Superball

In his search for a new synthetic, chemist Norman Stingley discovered something else. In one of his experiments he produced a rubbery material with unusual properties. When dropped on the floor it ricochetted straight back. The super-springy stuff bounced time after time, higher and faster than other materials.

Stingley named his discovery Zectron. His employers showed no interest in his invention, so in 1965 he brought a sample to Wham-O, the toy company that made Hula-Hoops and Frisbees. Wham-O bought the rights to Zectron and marketed it as Superball. In the first six months, Wham-O sold over 7 million Superballs and started a world-wide bouncing craze.

Teddy Bear

A hunting trip, a bear cub, and a cartoon started this stuffed toy fad. In 1902 Theodore "Teddy" Roosevelt, President of the United States, took a hunting trip in Mississippi. His hosts wanted him to return with a trophy, so they captured a bear cub for him to shoot. Roosevelt refused. A cartoonist working for the *Washington Star* drew a cartoon showing the president, a rifle in one hand, turning his back on the bear cub.

That gave toy salesman Morris Michtom the idea of creating a stuffed bear cub. To promote the toy he placed the cub and the cartoon in a toy-store window. Eager customers soon wanted to buy their own Teddy Bear. Other toy manufacturers began making stuffed bears, too, and in no time Teddy Bears became popular with children and adults alike.

ANSWERS TO NAME THESE TOYS:
1. Frisbee 2. Silly Putty 3. Lego 4. Yo-yo

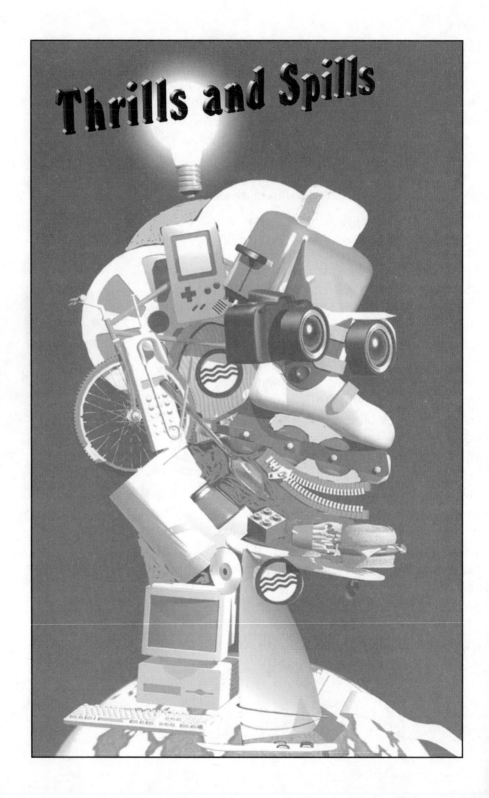

Thrills and Spills

THRILLS AND SPILLS

Name These Daredevil Inventions:

1. Start by attaching rollerskates to waterskis. Modify the design, add a few new features, and you'll have this popular land surfer.

2. George Nissen loved bouncing so much that he made the first of these from the metal frame of his own bed.

3. The Russians built the first track; the French attached wheels; Americans revived the fad and added curves, loops, and dips. Today, almost every major amusement park has one of these.

4. Inventor Armand Bombardier rigged an airplane propeller to a car motor and mounted the works onto the back of his family's sleigh to create this popular winter vehicle.

5. Invented by a Frenchman during World War II in order to weaken the German forces, this device opened up a new world of undersea adventure.

Answers on page 131.

The passengers on the first untethered hot air balloon flight (in 1783) were a duck, a sheep, and a rooster.

Mountain Bike

The bicycle as we know it as been around a long time. Back in 1839 Scottish blacksmith Kirkpatrick Macmillan built the first one by rigging two wheels to a frame and attaching pedals to the rear wheel. To demonstrate his bicycle he pedalled it around the countryside, covering 112 kilometres in just 10 hours. He might have gone further if it weren't for an accident. Kirkpatrick knocked down a young lady and was jailed for dangerous driving.

Bicycle designs have changed over the years. In the

1970s two styles were common. Adults rode racing bikes with curved handlebars, thin tires, and multiple gears. Racing bikes were best on the open road. They achieved high speeds and tackled steep slopes with ease. On rough ground, though, they were impractical, often becoming mired in dirt and mud. Kids preferred BMX (Bicycle Motor Cross) bikes. With their thick tires and small, sturdy frames, BMX bikes could handle bumpy hills and muddy trails easily. The BMX had one problem, however. With just one gear, pedalling uphill could be a difficult task.

Many people credit bicycle frame builder Joe Breeze with the next step in bicycle design. He combined features of both bicycles. He started with an adult-sized steel frame, then added thick balloon tires, a flat handlebar, handbrakes, and a gear system and deraileur. On smooth streets the new bike rode like a touring bike. Off road it easily tackled ruts and hills. The mountain bike had arrived.

At first, people were reluctant to try the mountain bike. With its bulging tires and wide handlebars, many thought it looked slow and clumsy. After trying it, though, they were won over by its versatility. Today, as much at home on city streets as on rugged hillsides, mountain bikes outsell all other styles.

Roller Coaster

Winters are long and cold in Russia, so it's natural that its people would take a liking to a new winter ride. In the 1600s "ice sliding" became the rage. High, sloped wooden ramps over twenty metres tall were built. Water, poured down the ramp, froze into a slick sheet of ice. To catch a ride people would trudge up a ladder, scramble onto a wooden sled, and shoot down the icy track at lightning speed.

It took 200 years, however, for the idea to catch on

elsewhere. In the 1800s a travelling Frenchmen was so impressed with Russian ice slides that he tried to build one in France. French winters were too mild to keep ice frozen, though, so he adapted the idea. He installed rollers down the centre of a wooden ramp for one-passenger sleds to ride down. The ride was slow and lacked thrills, but people loved the concept.

The first modern-looking roller coaster, called The Russian Mountains, was built in Paris in 1804. It had a wide track with a steep incline, and used sleds with wheels on the bottom. The new design permitted faster speeds and bigger thrills.

Other roller coasters appeared around France, each one larger and more exciting than the next. On one, the Centrifugal Pleasure Railway, riders swooped down a track, then went through a loop that turned them upside down before finishing in a straight stretch. For almost fifty years roller coasters flourished in France. Then, for some unknown reason, the fad died.

Much later they made a comeback, this time in the United States. America's first roller coaster was actually an abandoned rail line alongside a mountain in Pennsylvania. The Mauch Chunk Switchback was a coal-mining train that carried coal from the top of Sharp Mountain to the village below. The rail line was closed in 1870, but the tracks were put to good use. A steam engine at the top of the mountain hauled the cars uphill, then released them to coast to the bottom.

The ride grew so popular that soon other versions of the roller coaster appeared around the country. Each one offered something new: a longer track, more speed, dips, curves, twists, and loops. Today almost every major amusement park features one of these pulse-pounding rides.

Roller Skates

One day in 1760 Joseph Merlin carefully dressed for a London costume party. Merlin was a master craftsman, an inventor of musical instruments . . . and a bit of a show-off. He wanted people to notice him at the party.

He donned a clumsy costume, then strapped his latest invention to his feet — a pair of shoes with wheels — and made a grand entrance, rolling into the ballroom playing a violin. People noticed his colourful costume and heard the graceful tones of his violin, but mostly they saw him soar out of control across the ballroom as he realized, too late, that he could not turn or brake. He slammed into a large, expensive mirror, shattering it, smashing his violin, and severely injuring himself.

Each of Merlin's skates had two wheels, one in the front and one in the back. Over the next hundred years, other inventors tried to improve on Merlin's design by adding extra wheels or changing their position on the shoe. Despite the improvements, the problem of braking and turning remained, and roller-skating was more dangerous than fun.

Then in 1863 James Plimpton, an American furniture maker and inventor, took an interest in the wheeled shoes. He designed a skate that used four wheels, two in the front, and two in the back. He added rubber cushions between the axles and the metal base plate. By shifting weight and leaning to the side, a skater could steer and control the movement of his skates.

At first Plimpton merely wanted to make a skate that could be used during the summer as a substitute for ice skating. He enjoyed his invention so much, however, that he decided others should try his roller skates too. In 1867 he opened the world's first roller skating rink in Newport, Rhode Island. It was a wild success, with people swarming to it, eager to strap on a pair of Plimpton skates. As early as the 1890s dozens of rinks had opened across North America and Europe.

IN-LINE SKATES

In-Line Skates — A Not-So-New Invention

Sometimes it takes centuries for an idea to take hold. Take in-line skating as one example. This "new" invention has been three centuries in the making. Although Joseph Merlin is the first person known to use roller skates, most experts believe they were invented earlier, likely in Holland sometime in the 1700s, using wooden spools arranged in a row or line.

In 1823 inventor Robert John Tylers introduced a skate that used five wheels in a single line. Because the wheels in the centre were larger, the skater could steer by rocking back and forth. Tyler also rigged a type of braking system to his skates using hooks in the front and rear. But despite the obvious advantages of Tylers's skate, the in-line design never caught on. Most people were familiar only with the Plimpton style which used two pairs of parallel wheels.

Then in 1979 a nineteen-year-old semi-pro hockey player named Scott Olson happened to be browsing in a sporting goods store with his brother when he came across a pair of in-line skates. He figured he could keep up the training program he normally abandoned in the off season. When Olson showed the skates to his teammates, they liked them too, so he returned to the store and bought the entire supply.

In his spare time Olson refined the wheel and frame design and started manufacturing his own skates from the basement of his home. At first he sold in-line skates door-to-door, but as demand increased he quit skating and started his own company. Olson called his product the Ultimate Street Skate. Buyers called them Rollerblades. Olson eventually adopted the new name, signing the trademark to make it official.

In 1984 Scott Olson sold his company. The new owner kept the name Rollerblade, and launched an ambitious advertising campaign. With twenty-five skaters wearing black and neon outfits, the Rock 'n' Rollerblade Tour visited many towns and cities, performing stunts and dances. As the popularity of in-line skating spread, other manufacturers jumped on board, and today there are dozens of brands to choose from and sales of almost $500 million a year.

Scuba Diving

In the Second World War German forces occupied France, and German ships plied coastal waters, transporting soldiers and supplies. French resistance fighters struggled in secret to regain control of their country. One French naval officer and diver named Jacques-Yves Cousteau thought of a way to help bring the war to an end: use undersea divers to sabotage German ships.

The idea was sound, but not practical given the cumbersome gear divers used: heavy boots, bulky diving suits, and sealed helmets shaped like goldfish bowls. The diver breathed through tubes connected to a pump on board a nearby ship. The apparatus limited movement and made detection easy.

What was needed, Cousteau decided, was a portable diving device. Get rid of the tangled hoses and awkward diving gear and strap pressurized tanks of air to the diver's back instead. Give him a lightweight diving suit and rubber flippers. Let him swim like a fish. But Cousteau knew his device needed some way of regulating air pressure so that it would automatically match the increasing water pressure as the diver went deeper.

In 1942 Cousteau teamed up with engineer Emile Gagnon, who had invented control valves for various automobiles. The two adapted the valve design and rigged it to a cylinder of pressurized air. To try it out, Cousteau secretly tested it in a water tank in Paris. The valves controlled the flow of air as planned. But would it work in the rough and tumble depths of the sea? There was only one way to find out.

Jules Verne, a nineteenth-century science fiction writer, described the submarine decades before it was ever built.

One June morning in 1943, on a stretch of hidden shoreline along the French Riviera, Cousteau strapped on an air cylinder, donned flippers and a mask, adjusted the regulator, and plunged into the choppy waters. On shore, his wife and friends watched and waited anxiously.

Cousteau dove deep. Air from the cylinder flowed evenly. When he inhaled, the intake valve opened, allowing air to flow from the tank to his mouth. When he exhaled, an outlet valve shut off the air supply and allowed air to escape to the surface. The regulator controlled the air pressure, matching it to the surrounding water pressure.

Excited by the results, Cousteau made other dives, each deeper than the one before. The portable breathing apparatus allowed complete freedom underwater and revolutionized undersea exploration. Cousteau called his device the Aqualung. Others named it SCUBA for Self-Contained Underwater Breathing Apparatus.

Jacques-Yves Cousteau did more than invent the Aqualung. He opened up a whole new world of wonders to people around the globe.

He designed Conshelf, the first of several underwater habitats capable of sheltering divers for long periods of time.

He helped invent a two-person diving saucer. Powered by water jets and equipped with outside mechanical arms, the saucer took divers to a depth of 300 metres.

He pioneered undersea television, entertaining and educating people with programs about sunken ships, fish, and other undersea phenomena.

Skateboard

Something borrowed . . . something new . . . That pretty much sums up the story of the skateboard.

Surfboarding was one of the most popular sports of the 1950s. With conditions just right, the thrill of riding the waves couldn't be beat. But when the ocean was too rough or too calm, surfing was impossible, and disappointed surfers could only dream of better days.

One land-locked surfer in a little California beach town had an idea. He took a water ski and nailed an old roller skate to the bottom of it, then rode it downhill in much the same way as he would ride his surfboard down a wave.

The invention worked . . . for awhile. The rider surfed down the hill for a short distance, then lost control and crashed into the pavement. With more practice, and lots of bandages to cover his scratches and scrapes, the surfer got better.

Just who was the first skateboarder? No one knows

for certain, but many people credit Hobie Alter, a championship surfer, with the invention. Alter experimented with hardwood boards and roller skate wheels in the 1950s, hoping to find the perfect combination for a safe yet thrilling ride. At first he tried steel roller skate wheels, but these slipped and bounced out of control. He switched to "clay" wheels, the kind used on rink roller skates of the time, for a softer, smoother, more controlled ride.

Alter toured California beach towns demonstrating his skateboards. Other surfers like the idea, and it soon spread to sidewalks, streets, and parking lots everywhere.

Snowmobile

When Armand Bombardier's father gave him a car, he was pleased and thankful. So thankful, in fact, that he promptly yanked the motor out of it.

Bombardier loved machinery and was a genius when it came to fixing things. For a long time an idea had simmered in his mind. Valcourt, Quebec, the tiny town where he lived, received so much snow each winter that buildings and roads lay buried under huge drifts. Travel was impossible. What people needed, Bombardier decided, was a machine that rode above the snow. He rigged the car motor to the back of the family sleigh, then attached an old airplane propeller to it. When he cranked up the motor, the whirling propeller pushed the sleigh forward. At full throttle, the contraption flew over the snow.

Bombardier built his first snowmobile in 1922 when he was only fifteen, but it was rickety and dangerous, and his father ordered it dismantled. Not one to be discouraged, he spent years making the snowmobile safer and more practical. In 1928 he created an improved model using an automobile frame with skis in place of the front tires. Instead of

a propeller, four wheels at the back moved rubber belts that gripped the snow and pushed the machine forward. In 1937 he received a patent and started the Bombardier Snowmobile Company.

In the beginning his snowmobiles were bulky enclosed machines that resembled buses on skis. The largest of these, the B-12, was driven by a Ford V-8 engine and carried twelve passengers. In 1959 Bombardier made a smaller, lighter model that used a two-stroke engine, was pushed by a single wide belt, and carried one or two passengers. Believing this snowmobile would replace dogsleds used in the far north, Bombardier called it the Ski-Dog, then eventually renamed it the Ski-Doo.

The Ski-Doo revolutionized the snowmobile industry. Small and maneuverable, it provided fun and reliable transportation for snow-bound travellers around the world. Armand Bombardier, ever the tinkerer, continued to perfect his invention right up until his death in 1964.

Trampoline

Anyone who has ever jumped up and down on a bed knows what fun it can be. In fact, in the 1920s George Nissen invented a device to make it even more fun — the trampoline. Nissen's invention was not new in the usual sense. Clowns and circus performers had used "bouncing tables" in their acts for some time. But Nissen took the idea, made it practical, and put it in homes and gyms around the world.

Young Nissen started by emptying his father's garage, and scouring the town dump for parts: springs, scraps of iron, bits of rubber tubing, even an old sewing machine. Then, using a metal frame from his own bed, he attached ropes and strips of rubber, and covered the surface with canvas.

Most adults thought Nissen's invention was peculiar, but children loved it. When he set up his invention at a local camp, kids ignored the other equipment and lined up for their turn to bounce.

Nissen improved his trampoline by redesigning it, adjusting the springs and frame, making it sturdier and bouncier. As other people began to take an interest in it, he built a machine to mass produce it. But sales were slow. Most sporting goods dealers thought the trampoline was a gimmick, good for circus performers but not suitable for the general public. Nissen knew he had to change their attitude if his invention was to be successful.

He took out ads in magazines. He strapped a trampoline to his car and set up demonstrations at fairs and exhibitions. Slowly he convinced others of the trampoline's fitness potential. His strategies worked. By the late 1940s trampolines had become common equipment in gyms, and trampolining was accepted as an event in gymnastic competitions. Nowadays trampolines are lighter, safer, and more portable than ever, providing the young and young-at-heart with hours of bouncing pleasure.

In the 1400s Leonardo da Vinci drew plans for a helicopter. It wasn't built for another 500 years.

Windsurfer

Who says disagreements are bad? Not Hoyle Schweitzer or Jim Drake. An argument between the two friends in the 1960s started a new sport sensation. Surfing, Schweitzer said, wasted too much time. Surfers had to wait for the right waves, plus put up with crowds of other surfers along the beach. Sailing was a better sport.

Sailing, Drake said, was too complicated and

expensive. Surfing was simpler and easier to learn.

Instead of arguing further, the two men looked at the best features of each sport for a way to combine them into one. By attaching a sail to a surfboard they created the first sailing surfboard, or windsurfer.

Of course, it wasn't quite as simple as that. First they had to enlarge the surfboard to make room for both a standing person and a sail. Next they had to find some way to fasten the sail to the board. To solve the problem they invented a special fastener, a universal joint. It attached the sail to the board, but also allowed it to swivel, tilt, and even lie flat in the water.

Other changes were made too. Instead of a fibreglass board, the men switched to polyethylene, which was lighter, less expensive, and lasted longer. Straps were added to the top of the board to anchor the surfer's feet. Other features made the windsurfer more stable and easier to use.

The windsurfer rage spread quickly. One man who spotted a windsurfer in the water stopped his car, ran to the beach and ordered six boards on the spot. Even the experts were thrilled with the invention. They called it the first original sailing idea in over one hundred years.

Spotlight On Invention

Adapt an Existing Invention and Use It for a New or Different Purpose

*Minds are like parachutes.
They only function when open.*

— Anonymous

THE STORY OF THE FIRST WATERSKIS

How Winter Visited Summer in Minnesota

Ralph Samuelson was an avid snow skier living in Lake City, Minnesota. When the summer of 1920 rolled around, the eighteen-year-old started looking for a replacement for his favourite winter sport. One day, on a whim, he lugged his snow skis to the lake. He attached a thirty-metre rope to a boat, strapped on the skis and ordered the boat driver to gun the engine. The boat lurched forward, hauling Samuelson behind it. But the skis were too narrow and the boat couldn't go fast enough. Instead of riding on top of the water, Samuelson was dragged through it.

Not one to give up, he set to work designing a better ski. He found an oak barrel and dismantled it, then took two of its curved staves and attached them to his feet. The staves kept him afloat, but the front tips kept catching the waves and tripping him headfirst into the lake.

On his next attempt he boiled two pine boards in water and clamped the softened wood to curved moulds. When the boards dried, they kept the curved shape. The new skis worked better. The wide boards supported Samuelson on the water, and the longer curves sliced through the waves gracefully. But the boat was still slow. At a top speed of only thirty-two kilometres an hour, Samuelson had difficulty staying afloat.

The first Jeep was built in 1941. It was designed to carry four soldiers low enough to dodge enemy fire.

He improved the skis further, making them longer and even wider. He used steel straps at the tip for extra strength, and glued rubber padding on the boards to keep his feet secure. Samuelson changed the tow rope too, adding a rubber-coated metal ring as a handle grip. Next he replaced the boat's motor with a more powerful 220-horsepower one that reached speeds almost twice as fast.

With these improvements, Samuelson flew over the water. Word soon spread around Lake City, and before long spectators gathered to watch him practise his newly invented sport. Today waterskiing is a favourite summer pastime around the globe.

MORE ABOUT INVENTOR RALPH SAMUELSON

Samuelson did not become rich from his invention. He made skis only for his own use, and often gave free one-man water shows. The first commercial water skis were patented in 1925 by another inventor, Fred Walker of Huntington, New York.

The first earmuffs were created in 1873 after the inventor, Chester Greenwood, froze his ears while skating.

Besides inventing water skis, Ralph Samuelson discovered many of the techniques that are used by today's water-skiers. Because the boat towing him moved slowly, Samuelson learned to boost his speed and stay afloat by zig-zagging back and forth behind the boat.

Always the daredevil, Samuelson also invented the first water-ski jump. He built a wooden ramp, smeared it with greasy pork fat, and anchored it in the lake. At top speed he sailed almost fifty metres over the ramp before making graceful landings in the water.

Parasailing had not been invented yet, but that didn't stop Samuelson from accidentally devising his own version of this sport. To gain speed, he once rigged an airplane propeller to a boat. The boat raced across the lake at high speeds, lifting him high in the air.

There are many modern variations of Samuelson's invention. Nowadays jet skis rip across the water, and power boats often tow kneeboards, discs, mini-surfboards, or sleds.

Other Inventions Created by Adapting an Existing Invention

Tea Bag Thomas Sullivan owned a tea importing business in New York City in the early 1900s. To promote sales he shipped customers small samples of tea leaves in metal containers. In 1904, when the price of metal skyrocketed, Sullivan could no longer afford to use the containers. To take their place, he made small bags out of silk and stuffed them with tea leaves. But his customers misunderstood their purpose. Instead of slitting the bags and dumping the loose tea into a pot to brew, they started dunking the whole bag into the boiling water. They liked the mess-free convenience of the bags, and swamped Sullivan with orders for more.

Toothpaste Tube Toothpaste was once sold in jars. People simply dipped their toothbrushes into the paste whenever they wanted to brush. In 1892 Dr. Washington Wentworth Sheffield thought of a better idea. He noticed that artists bought oil paints in metal tubes. Why not use similar tubes for toothpaste? he asked. He copied the tube design, filling it with toothpaste instead of paint. People loved the convenience and cleanliness, and the idea caught on right away.

Tupperware When Earl Tupper, a chemist and businessman, wanted to make an airtight plastic container, he studied a paint can and adapted its design. The can had a flared rim and tight-fitting lid that locked into place, features he added to his Tupperware food storage containers.

It took the Nestlé Company from 1931 to 1938 to find the formula for instant coffee.

The dashboard air bag was invented by R.H. Hodges in 1953, but wasn't installed in cars until 1981.

Earth to Space to Earth!

Putting people into space is no easy trick. It takes new technology and stronger, lighter materials. But astronauts are not the only ones who benefit. Since the start of the space program in the 1950s, several space inventions have found new life here on earth:

Metallic Balloons More than just pretty and durable, the light, shiny fabric in metallic balloons was originally developed as reflective insulating material for spacesuits and spacecraft.

Joystick The original joystick was used on the Lunar Rover, the vehicle astronauts drove on the moon's surface in the Apollo landings. With it, astronauts could steer and accelerate with just one hand. Today joysticks are used by handicapped drivers as well as video game lovers.

Portable Refrigeration Units Ordinary refrigeration coils and compressors were too bulky for use in space, so NASA scientists developed a solid-state replacement called a thermo-electric module. No larger than a matchbook and powered by only a few amps of electricity, the module is used today in cooler-style portable refrigeration units that plug into the cigarette lighter of a car.

OTHER INVENTIONS THAT THRILL

Parachute

For centuries people have dreamed of falling peacefully through the air from high places. In 1494 Leonardo da Vinci drew plans for a tent-like parachute and wrote about how it would work, but he never built one. The first recorded jump with a parachute was made in 1783. Joseph Montgolfier strapped a parachute to his waist and jumped off a tall building in Paris. He saw the parachute as a safety device, a way for people to escape from burning buildings. But it wasn't until hot air balloons and airplanes came into use that the parachute became popular.

Powerboats and Outboard Motors

One hot summer day in 1907 Ole Evinrude, a Wisconsin machinist, set out on a romantic picnic with his sweetheart, Bessie. They packed a lunch, hopped aboard a rowboat, and headed across Lake Michigan to a secluded island. Once there, Bessie asked for ice cream. Evinrude, eager to impress, rowed back to shore to get it, then back again to the island to deliver it.

The trip took so long that the ice cream was a puddle by the time Bessie received it. Clearly a faster means of travel was needed, Evinrude thought. He designed a one-cylinder 1.5-horsepower motor that attached to the back of the boat. The outboard motor was instantly popular and made powerboating both appealing and affordable. Eventually Evinrude married Bessie and the two went into business making and selling Evinrudes.

Answers to Name These Daredevil Inventions:
1. Skateboard 2. Trampoline 3. Roller coaster 4. Snowmobile
5. SCUBA diving gear

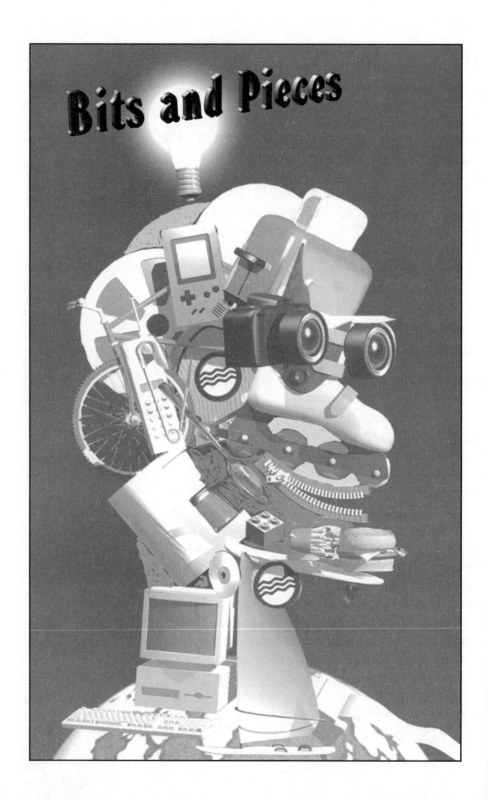

BITS AND PIECES

Name These Small but Useful Inventions:

1. Some people use them to spread glue; others to dust delicate furniture. Most, though, use them just the way inventor Leo Gerstenzang intended: to clean hard-to-reach body parts.

2. So simple (a single piece of wire) and so common (every closet has dozens), yet Albert Parkhouse never made a penny from his invention.

3. Josephine Dickson was a bit of a klutz. Her husband, Earl, came to her rescue with his invention: a sticky, ready-to-use skin patch.

4. Fed up with laces, buttons, hooks, and clips, Whitcomb Judson invented this quicker "takes-one-hand-only" fastener.

5. For the first time, no dipping, refilling, or blotting! The Biro brothers figured their invention was a winner, but it took World War II pilots to prove just how well it worked.

Answers on page 148.

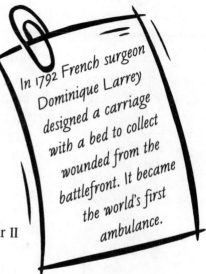

In 1792 French surgeon Dominique Larrey designed a carriage with a bed to collect wounded from the battlefront. It became the world's first ambulance.

Band-Aid

Josephine Dickson was accident prone. Only one week into her marriage, she had already cut herself twice with a kitchen knife. To bandage her cuts she called upon her husband, Earl, for help. Earl worked for Johnson & Johnson, a company that produced surgical tape and gauze. He had plenty of practical experience with bandages so he faithfully patched up his wife's wounds.

But Earl began to worry that Josephine might cut herself while he was at work, so he began to experiment. He cut a strip of surgical tape and laid it out on a table. Next he folded a strip of gauze and placed it in the middle of the tape. To keep the ends fresh and sticky, he covered them with pieces of fabric. Now Josephine had a convenient, ready-to-use bandage. Should she cut herself, she could easily tear off the fabric and stick the gauze over the wound.

Earl Dickson showed his invention to the people at Johnson & Johnson. They liked it and in 1920 began to market the bandage. They named it the Band-Aid: "band" for tape, and "aid" for first-aid.

Ballpoint Pen

Painter, sculptor, hypnotist, journalist. Ladislao Biro was all of these, a busy and talented man. So busy that even refilling a fountain pen seemed like a waste of time.

In 1935 Biro worked as an editor for a small newspaper in Hungary, using a fountain pen to write and correct articles. The sharp nib often scratched and ripped the paper. The pen left ink blobs on the page, and much of Biro's time went to cleaning up the mess and refilling the pen with ink. What he needed, he decided, was a pen that held its own supply of ink, one that wrote smoothly, without smears and smudges or tears in the paper.

The idea seemed simple. The actual invention was not. With his brother, Georg, a chemist, Biro set about redesigning the fountain pen. Instead of a sharp nib they put a tiny rolling metal ball in the tip. Then they filled the pen with thick ink and sealed the cylinder. It was a fabulous failure. The ink flowed unevenly, skipping in some spots, leaving blobs in others. Because the pen relied on gravity to spread ink on the roller ball, it only worked when held straight up.

The Biros tried again. This time they replaced the

smooth metal ball with a rougher one. The new ball acted like a sponge, lapping up ink as it rolled across the page. The pen wrote more smoothly and evenly, and even worked when held at a slant. But it was expensive, and most people would not spend money on such a luxury.

Then, during World War II, sales took an unexpected jump. Airforce pilots discovered the Biros's invention. Unlike fountain pens, which relied on gravity and had to be refilled, the ballpoint pen wrote well at high altitudes. Word of the "miracle pen" spread quickly. In October, 1945, the first ballpoint pens went on sale in New York. Thousands of customers squeezed into a department store, anxious to be among the first to own one. Even at a cost of $12.50 each, the entire stock of 10,000 pens sold in a single day.

Crayola Crayons

At least half of all children between the ages of two and seven will pick up a wax crayon today. On average they'll each spend twenty-seven minutes colouring. Kids have been colouring and drawing with waxy sticks throughout history, but the wax crayon got a boost in popularity when the Binney and Smith Company joined the crayon business in 1903.

Originally Binney and Smith sold charcoal and red barn paint. Later they sold a new type of slate pencil to schools. When company officials visited classrooms hoping to drum up business for their pencils, they noticed children hunched over papers, clutching stubby wax crayons. The colours were blotchy and inconsistent. The crayons were brittle, too, often shattering in the little hands holding them.

Figuring they could do better, Binney and Smith started experimenting with wax and pigments. Batches of oily wax were melted and churned by

PEN FACTS

Marcel Bich wanted to produce high-quality ballpoint pens at an affordable price. For two years the French businessman studied every ballpoint pen on the market. In 1945 he started manufacturing a clear plastic, non-leaky, inexpensive pen in a shed outside Paris. He called his product the Bic. The pen was so popular and affordable that soon millions were being produced each day.

Wax crayons have a distinctive smell. In fact, crayons are one of the most readily recognized of all smells. Why? It's because of the stearic acid in the beef fat that is used to manufacture crayons.

Take all the Crayola crayons produced in a single year, melt them together and what do you get? A giant crayon, bigger than the Statue of Liberty, that stands 125 metres tall and is 37 metres around!

In 1996 Binney and Smith manufactured their 100 billionth Crayola crayon. To celebrate, they invented a special, one-of-a-kind colour, named Blue Ribbon. Though many of their sets now contain Blue Ribbn crayons, the actual 100 billionth crayon they made is a collector's item valued at $100,000.

hand, tinted with various additives, then poured into moulds and allowed to harden. Eventually Binney and Smith had a durable, colour-consistent crayon that could be sold at a reasonable price.

Alice Binney, wife of Edwin Binney (one of the company founders) and a schoolteacher herself, gave the new product its name. She combined the French word *craie* meaning "stick of colour" with *ola* meaning "oily" and called the crayons Crayola.

The first boxes of Crayola crayons cost five cents and contained eight colours: red, blue, green, yellow, orange, brown, violet, and black. Today, they offer seventy-two colour choices and manufacture over two billion Crayola crayons each year.

Drinking Straw

For thousands of years people have used hollow reeds and grasses to slurp their favourite drinks. Until 1888, that is. That's when Marvin Stone invented something better.

Stone operated a factory in Washington, D.C. that made paper cigarette holders. After a hard day at work he liked to visit his local tavern for a cool drink. The tavern kept a supply of natural straws — hollow stalks of grass — for people who preferred to down their drinks that way. The hollow stalks worked, but softened with use and left a grassy taste behind.

One day Stone, noticing that the paper cigarette holders he produced were similar to straws, had an idea. He wound long strips of paper around pencils and glued the ends together. Then he passed several of his paper straws to the tavern owner. Each time Stone ordered a drink, the owner handed him a paper straw. Before long, other customers took notice and wanted their own.

Figuring he was on to something good, Stone worked on his straw design. He found an ideal length (just long enough to reach the bottom of most glasses), adjusted the width so that pits and pulp in the drink would not become lodged in it, and coated the paper with wax to make the straw last longer. Finally, he patented his invention and went into production.

People liked Stone's straw! Because they did not have to lift glasses to their lips, their drinks stayed cold longer. Plus, a paper straw left no aftertaste and its waxy coating kept it firm for a long time. It was convenient and hygienic too.

Kleenex

When World War I caused a shortage of cotton, the Kimberly-Clark Company looked for a paper substitute. Using cellulose from wood pulp and a small amount of cotton, they made an absorbent product called Cellucotton, but when the war ended, huge quantities of Cellucotton were left over. Kimberly-Clark looked for new ways to sell the stuff.

Tired of her daughter's leaky diapers, Marion Donovan lined a plastic envelope with absorbent material to create the first disposable diaper in 1951.

In 1924 Kimberly-Clark introduced a new cellulose product — disposable paper sheets for removing make-up and cold cream. At sixty-five cents a box, big money in those days, it sold poorly.

The company tried a number of marketing strategies. They invented a "pop-up" box and offered sheets in a variety of colours. They even gave their product a short, snappy name: Kleenex.

Sales started to increase and mail poured into the company offices. Surprisingly, people wrote praising Kleenex, not because they found it handy for removing make-up, but because they liked using it as a disposable handkerchief.

Confused, the marketing people at Kimberly-Clark went to Peoria, Illinois, to study the situation. They passed out coupons to a group of Kleenex users. One coupon said: "We pay to prove there is no way like Kleenex to remove cold cream." Another coupon said: "We pay to prove Kleenex is wonderful for handkerchiefs." By turning in one of the coupons, people cast their vote telling how they used Kleenex. The study showed that most people didn't use it for removing make-up. More than sixty-one percent used Kleenex just to wipe noses and stifle sneezes.

The company quickly changed the slant of its advertising. Using the slogan "Don't put a cold in your pocket," they sold Kleenex as a disposable handkerchief. Sales multiplied, and soon "Pass me a Kleenex, please," became a phrase used in homes across the country.

Liquid Paper

Bette Nesmith Graham, an executive secretary at a Dallas bank, was a lousy typist. She made so many mistakes that her work was smudged from constant erasing. But one day in 1951 she discovered a solution to her typing problem. "I remembered trying to make a little extra money by helping design the holiday windows at the bank," she said later. "With lettering, an artist never corrects by erasing, but always paints over the error. So I decided to use what artists use."

She mixed some tempera paint in a bottle. Then using a small brush, she painted over her typing mistakes. The trick worked. She kept a bottle of white paint in her desk drawer, and made smudge-free corrections quickly and easily.

Graham wanted to keep her trick a secret, though. She felt sneaky. After all, she figured, wasn't she passing herself off as a better typist than she really was? But word of her magic formula spread around the bank. Other secretaries begged for their own supply. Graham mixed and bottled batches at home, then sold bottles around the office.

LIQUID PAPER FACTS

In the early years of her business, Graham worked days at her secretarial job, and nights and weekends making Liquid Paper. That ended the morning she made a mistake that got her fired. Instead of typing her employer's name at the bottom of a letter, she accidentally typed "The Liquid Paper Company."

In 1979 Graham sold her company to the Gillette Corporation for $47.5 million. In addition, Gillette agreed to pay royalties on each bottle sold until the year 2000.

In 1956 she decided to expand her business. First, though, she needed to improve her product. She went to the library to research tempera paints, sought advice from a high school chemistry teacher, and even had a man from a paint manufacturing plant show her how to grind and mix paint. Eventually she produced a quick-drying, hard-to-detect liquid. She patented her invention under the name Liquid Paper, and started her own manufacturing business.

At first business was slow. Then a national magazine wrote an article about the invention, and sales improved. Instead of selling only a hundred bottles a month, Graham started selling thousands. When her business outgrew the family garage the entire operation moved to larger quarters. Within ten years, Liquid Paper sales reached more than $1 million a year, and production increased to 10,000 bottles a day. By 1975, the company was producing 25 million bottles a year. From a single bottle of paint hidden in her desk drawer, Bette Nesmith Graham started a business empire that changed the writing habits of people around the world.

To make scratch 'n' sniff stickers, tiny droplets of scent are sprayed onto paper, then sealed with a thin layer of plastic resin. Scratching breaks the surface and releases the scent.

Nowadays computers have eliminated some of our need for correction fluids like Liquid Paper. With computers, errors are simply corrected on-screen before documents are printed. But there are still times when we use pens or markers, and for those occasions Bette Nesmith Graham's dip and dab invention proves indispensible.

Pencil

A simple thing, the pencil. A slender wooden tube, fitted with a black core, topped with an eraser.

But with a single pencil you can draw a line over 50 kilometres long, or write 45,000 words. Simple, but effective.

The modern pencil got its start in 1564 during a wild winter storm in England. A huge oak tree toppled over. Beneath its roots, local farmers discovered a black substance they mistakenly thought was lead. The "lead" was excellent for drawing and writing, but it left smudges and smears. To solve the problem of messy hands, splinters of the black substance were wrapped with string. Later they were jammed into tubes of wood or leather.

In 1683 a man named J. Pettus created the first wooden pencil. He sliced a small stick of cedar lengthwise, hollowed out the middle, fitted a rod of "lead" inside, then glued the two halves together.

In 1779, more than two centuries after "lead's" discovery, a scientist determined that the substance under the oak tree was not lead at all, but a form of carbon. He named it graphite, from a Greek work *graphein*, meaning "to write." Wrong though it was, people continued to use the name lead pencils, a term still in use today.

PENCIL FACTS

Ever wonder about the numbers stamped on a pencil? They indicate the hardness of the graphite mixture. The lower the number, the more graphite it contains, the softer it is, and the darker it writes.

Make a mistake? Erase it with a piece of bread! That's what the earliest pencil users did. It was only in 1752 that the first rubber eraser came into being.

Over 2 billion pencils are sold each year in North America alone.

Post-It Notes

Spencer Silver figured his experiment was a failure. So did other scientists who worked for the Minnesota Mining and Manufacturing Company (3M) in 1970.

Silver had tried to invent a new super-strong glue. Instead the batch he mixed was the opposite, super-weak. The glue barely stuck, and it was so temporary that two objects could be peeled apart easily. Silver's glue was shelved and almost forgotten.

Then one Sunday, four years later, an idea struck another 3M scientist, Arthur Fry. Fry was singing in his church choir. He often used bits of paper to mark his place in his choir book, but they would fall out, so he kept losing his place. "I

don't know if it was a dull sermon or divine inspiration," Fry said, "but my mind began to wander and suddenly I thought of an adhesive that had been discovered several years earlier . . ."

When he returned to work the next day, Fry tried out his idea. He spread Spencer Silver's super-weak glue on bits of paper and stuck the markers to the pages of his book. The markers stayed in place, but separated with little effort.

For nearly a year and a half Fry perfected the glue, adjusting the formula so that the markers peeled off without leaving a residue. When he was ready, he passed out samples to his co-workers at 3M. They weren't impressed. No one was sure why people would buy sticky notepaper when ordinary notepaper sold for so much less.

In 1977 Post-It Notes, as the sticky pads were called, were test-marketed in four cities. In two cities, sales were poor. In the other two, sales were amazing. When 3M representatives looked more closely, they discovered the reason for the difference. In the two cities with terrific sales, dealers had passed out free samples. Once people had Post-Its in their hands, they discovered many different uses for them.

Today, Post-Its can be found in homes and offices, and on everything from refrigerators to TV screens, proving that even failures can be outstanding successes given the right circumstances.

Before postage stamps were introduced in 1840, people paid for their mail when it was delivered, not before it was sent.

Another Sticky Invention Thomas Alva Edison, one of America's greatest inventors, had a sticky problem to solve. Whenever he wanted to glue two pieces of paper together, he always ended up with glue on his hands. It was unpleasant, and cleaning up took valuable

LICK-AND-STICK

time. Edison told an assistant to spread glue on a piece of paper, then after it dried, to moisten it. The moisture made the glue sticky again. Edison's simple experiment revolutionized the glue industry. Today, envelopes and postage stamps still use Edison's simple lick-and-stick formula.

Q-Tips

Leo Gerstenzang, a Polish-American, was an observant man. As he watched his wife bathe their baby, he noticed her wrap a wad of absorbent cotton around a toothpick to clean the baby's ears and other hard-to-reach places. But preparing the swab took both of Mrs. Gerstenzang's hands, and all the while the baby squirmed and wriggled. Having a ready-made cotton swab might be a handy thing, Gerstenzang figured. He set out to invent an application that was safe and reliable; that is, the wooden stick would not splinter, the cotton would not fall off, and an equal amount of cotton would be attached to each end. To add to the convenience of the product, Gerstenzang packaged the swabs in a unique sliding tray so that a busy parent could open and remove a single swab with only one hand. He tested several names for his invention. Finally, in 1926, he found one that seemed just right: Q-Tips. The "Q" stood for "quality," and Gerstenzang decided that described his swab best.

People today use Q-Tips in all kinds of ways, from applying glues to dusting delicate furniture to spreading on make-up. Of course, as Leo Gerstenzang originally hoped, they use cotton swabs to clean baby, too.

Anne Moore noticed how some African mothers strapped children to their backs to carry them. She adapted the idea to invent the Snugli Infant Carrier.

Safety Pin

Walter Hunt had a talent for inventing. During his lifetime (1796-1859) he invented knife sharpeners, sewing machines, paraffin candles, fountain pens, gongs for fire engines, and dozens of other useful items. He also invented Antipodean Performers — suction shoes worn by circus performers to scale walls and walk across ceilings.

Hunt may have been a gifted inventor, but he was a poor businessman. He seldom patented his inventions and rarely profited from their use.

In 1849, Hunt owed money. He tried to pay off a $15 debt by doing what came most naturally to him, inventing something new. He took a piece of wire, twisted and bent it, and within three hours produced a pin with a clasp that enclosed the point and protected the wearer from being poked.

This time Hunt took out a patent on his invention. But with his creditors demanding payment, he decided to settle his debt quickly. He sold the rights to his invention for $400, paid off his debt, and congratulated himself that he had $385 to spare.

It's likely that Hunt felt less content when he watched his invention — the modern safety pin — sell by the millions, once again earning someone else the fortune he deserved.

SPOTLIGHT ON INVENTION

Borrow an Idea from Nature

Originality is simply a fresh pair of eyes.

— Woodrow Wilson

Only an inventor knows how to borrow, and every man is or should be an inventor.

— Ralph Waldo Emerson

THE STORY OF VELCRO

How a Nuisance of Nature Inspired an Inventor

One day in 1948 George de Mestral, a Swiss engineer, went on a hunting trip. As he wound his way over mountain trails, tiny burrs stuck to his socks and trousers. He stopped to pry off the sticky seeds, but found it was no easy task. Each burr clung stubbornly to his clothes, and freeing them took a lot of effort and patience.

De Mestral was curious. Just why were the burrs so hard to remove? When he looked at them up close, he noticed that each one had tiny hooks that latched onto the loops of thread in his clothing. His inventive mind began to churn. Why not make a fastener of loops and hooks that locked onto one another?

The idea was far simpler than the process. To make the fastener work, he needed two types of cloth, one with hooks, the other with loops. After some searching he found a weaver who would make the cloth by hand on a small loom. He eagerly tried out the first sample. It worked! The hooks locked into the loops. But to manufacture the fastener in bulk, a quicker method had to be found.

De Mestral experimented with many techniques: steam, hot air, ultrasonic sound, glue. After months of trial and error he found a way of making rigid loops of nylon thread.

Soon after, he found a way of cutting the loops to turn them into hooks. But it took a full eight years to develop the fastener and a machine that could make loops and hooks quickly. De Mestral called his fastener Velcro — Vel for velvet, cro for "*crochet*" or "small hook" in French.

144

With Velcro, parts can be joined and separated quickly and easily, time and time again. Today Velcro has hundreds of uses, from replacing snaps, buttons, and zippers in clothing, to attaching gear in space shuttles.

Other Inventions Inspired by Nature

Barbed Wire Joseph F. Glidden noticed how early settlers planted rows of thorny shrubs to keep their livestock from wandering. He adapted the idea, twisting steel "thorns" onto wire to make barbed wire.

Light-and-Sound Show A 1939 thunderstorm with booming thunder, and lightning streaking across the sky, illuminating a nearby castle, made quite an impression on Paul Robert-Houdin. The experience inspired him to produce the first "light-and-sound" show in 1953.

Pressurized Flight Suit Daredevil aviator Wiley Post wanted to set high-altitude speed records. To solve the problem of too little oxygen, he designed a pressurized rubber flight suit. Unfortunately, the suit was awkward and bulky. One day in 1934 Post spotted a tomato worm crawling across a leaf. He noticed its flexible joints and the way they helped the worm twist and crawl. This inspired him to add flexible sections to the joints of his flight suit to make it more comfortable and practical. Today his design is used by military pilots who fly at high altitudes. It's also the basis for space suits worn by astronauts.

See Also . . .
Pringles (page 19)
Ant Farm (page 98)

Zipper

Whitcomb Judson lost his patience when it came to doing up shoes and boots. Laces, buttons, hooks, and clips took too long to fasten. The constant tugging, tying, and bending over made his back stiff and fingers sore. Determined to find a better way, Judson came up with a new fastener. In 1893 he patented a "clasp locker and unlocker for shoes." His invention consisted of a movable slider that joined sets of hooks and eyes. Judson also invented a machine to mass produce the Clasp Locker, as he called the device.

Judson's invention didn't work well. It jammed, snapped, and often unfastened on its own. Most people stuck to their old-fashioned laces and buttons. Discouraged, but not beaten, Judson improved his fastener. In 1910 he was ready with a new model, called the C-Curity. Unfortunately, it was not much better than the Clasp Locker.

But Judson was on to something. One of his workers, Gideon Sunback, took an interest in the slide fastener. After nearly four years of improvement, Sunback produced a new slide fastener, one that worked smoothly and remained fastened.

Sales of the "hookless" fastener were still slow, however. Then in 1923 a rubber company produced a new type of boot. It featured a slide fastener rather than buttons or laces. Just "zip 'er up or zip 'er down," the company advertised. The catchy name stuck, and the popularity of Judson's invention soared. Today zippers are used in everything from clothing to backpacks, and everywhere from the remote Arctic to space shuttles orbiting the earth.

Canned food appeared in 1811, but can openers were not invented for another 44 years.

OTHER USEFUL BITS

Coat Hanger

Albert J. Parkhouse worked for a company that made wire lampshade frames. One day in 1903 he could not find a place to hang up his coat because all the hooks were taken. Rather than throw his coat on the floor, he grabbed some wire from the shop, gave it a twist or two, and in no time had a simple hanger. Unfortunately, his employer spotted his invention, took credit for the idea, and made a fortune from it, while Parkhouse continued to work for low wages in the factory.

Pull-Top Can

At a picnic in 1959 Ermal Cleon Fraze, a mechanical engineer, reached for a can of soda. But he had forgotten to bring a can opener. Desperate for a thirst-quenching drink, Fraze spent half an hour prying the can open on the bumper of his car. The experience gave him an idea. He invented a new can, one with a pull-top lid. Nowadays, almost all canned drinks are equipped with some form of Fraze's invention.

Refrigerator Magnet

John and Arlene Arnasto sold a line of decorator wall hooks. In 1964 Arlene got the idea that a hook for a refrigerator would be a good idea. John made one shaped like a tea kettle and with a small bell. To its back he added a small magnet so that the hook could be clipped in place and removed if necessary. When the hook proved to be a hot seller, the Arnastos added others to their line and started the refrigerator magnet craze.

Rubber Band

Hundreds of years ago natives of Central and South America discovered the rubber tree. When Europeans arrived, they discovered the wonders of rubber for themselves and used the sap to make hats, coats, toys, even crude rubber bottles.

When Englishman Thomas Hancock received a rubber bottle, he saw possibilities others had missed. He took a knife to it, sliced the bottle into rings, and invented the first rubber bands. Hancock used them in clothing to hold up stockings and pants, but he never bothered to take out a patent to protect his idea.

Twenty-five years later another Englishman, Stephen Perry, realized that rubber bands could be used in many other ways. Perry took out a patent on the invention and opened the world's first rubber-band factory.

The first eyeglasses were made in Venice, Italy, around 1281.

Benjamin Franklin invented bifocal eyeglasses in 1784.

Answers to Name These Small But Useful Inventions:
1. Q-Tips 2. Coat hanger 3. Band-aid 4. Zipper 5. Ballpoint pen

For Further Reading

Asseng, Nathan. *Better Mousetraps*. Minneapolis:
Lerner Publications Co., 1990.

Buchman, Dian Dincin & Groves, Seli. *What If?* New York:
Scholastic Inc., 1988.

Caney, Steven. *Steven Caney's Invention Book*. New York:
Workman Publishing, 1985.

Feldman, Anthony & P. Ford. *Scientists and Inventors*. New York:
Facts on File, 1979.

Flatow, Ira. *They All Laughed . . .* New York: Harper Collins, 1992.

Giscard d'Estaing, Valerie-Anne (ed.) *Inventions and Discoveries 1993.*
New York: Facts on File, 1993.

Jones, Charlotte Foltz. *Mistakes That Worked*. New York: Doubleday, 1991.

National Geographic. *Small Inventions That Made a Big Difference*. Washington,
D.C.: National Geographic Society, 1984.

Nostbakken, Janis & Humphrey, Jack. *The Canadian Inventors Book*. Toronto:
Greey de Pencier Publications, 1976.

Panati, Charles. *Extraordinary Origins of Everyday Things*. New York: Perennial
Library, 1987.

Reader's Digest. *The Inventions That Changed the World*. New York:
The Reader's Digest Association, Inc., 1982.

Reader's Digest. *Stories Behind Everyday Things*. New York:
The Reader's Digest Association, Inc., 1982.

Travers, Bridget (ed.) *World of Inventions*. Detroit: Gale Research Inc., 1994.

Vare, Ethlie Ann & Ptacek, Greg. *Mothers of Invention*. New York:
William Morrow & Co., Inc., 1988.

Verstraete, Larry. *The Serendipity Effect*. Toronto: Scholastic-TAB
Publications Ltd., 1989.

Wuffson, Don L. *Extraordinary Stories Behind the Invention of Ordinary Things.*
New York: Lothrop, Lee & Shepard Books, 1981.

INDEX

The following are brand names, registered trademarks, or patented names.

Alien Terrain Patrol
Alka-Seltzer
Animal Crackers
Antipodean Performer
Ant Farm
Band-Aid
Barbie Doll
Bic
Bingo
Birdseye
Biro
Blibber Blubber Bubble Gum
Brad's Drink
Brownie Camera
Calgon
Candyland
C-Curity
Celluloid
Clasp Locker
Cheerios
Chiclets
Coca-Cola
Coke
Cracker Jack
Crayola
Donkey Kong
Dubble Bubble
Duplo
Erector Set
Evinrude
Exxon
Frisbee
Frito-Lay
Gatorade
G.I. Joe
Googolplex

Hires Root Beer
Hula Hoop
IMAX
Ivory Soap
Jeep
JELL-O
Kellogg
Ken Doll
Kleenex
Kodak
Kraft Dinner
Lego
Lego Technic
Lifesavers
Lionel Train
Liquid Paper
Lincoln Logs
Magic Eye
Matchbox Toy
Mega Claw Excavator
Melitta
Monopoly
Mortal Kombat
Nestlé
Nike
Nintendo
Nutty Putty
Oreo
PacMan
Papermate
Ping Pong
Pepsi-Cola
Play-Doh
POG
Pong
PopTart
Post-It Notes
Pluto Platter
Pringles
Polaroid

Polaroid Land Camera
Pull-Top Lid
Q-Tips
Radarange
Rollerblades
Root Tea
Rubik's Cube
Scrabble
Scotchgard
SCUBA
Shredded Wheat
Silly Putty
Ski-Doo
Slinky
Snowmobile
Snakes and Ladders
Snugli Infant Carrier
Sony
S.O.S Pads
Superball
Super Mario Brothers
Teddy Bear
Teflon
Tinkertoy
Toastmaster
Trampoline
Trivial Pursuit
Tupperware
Twister
Velcro
Waffle Sole
Walkman
WD-40
Wham-O
Xerox
Zectron
Zipper
Zamboni
yo-yo